AS/A-LEVEL

STUDENT GUIDE

NATIONAL
EXTENSION
COLLEGE

PEARSON EDEXCEL

Religious Studies

Religion and ethics

Cressida Tweed and Amanda Forshaw

HODDER
EDUCATION
AN HACHETTE UK COMPANY

Hodder Education, an Hachette UK company, Blenheim Court, George Street, Banbury, Oxfordshire OX16 5BH

Orders

Bookpoint Ltd, 130 Park Drive, Milton Park, Abingdon, Oxfordshire OX14 4SB

tel: 01235 827827

fax: 01235 400401

e-mail: education@bookpoint.co.uk

Lines are open 9.00 a.m.–5.00 p.m., Monday to Saturday, with a 24-hour message answering service. You can also order through the Hodder Education website: www.hoddereducation.co.uk

This Student Guide draws on material developed by the National Extension College (NEC) for its A level Religious Studies course. The National Extension College is an educational charity and offers a wide range of GCSE and A level courses (www.nec.ac.uk).

ISBN 978-1-5104-3340-3

First printed 2019

Impression number 5 4 3 2

Year 2023 2022 2021 2020 2019

This Guide has been written specifically to support students preparing for the Pearson Edexcel AS and A-level Religious Studies examinations. The content has been neither approved nor endorsed by Pearson Edexcel and remains the sole responsibility of the authors.

Typeset by Integra Software Services Pvt. Ltd., Pondicherry, India

Printed in Italy

Cover photograph: Gordon J A Dixon/Shutterstock.com

Hachette UK's policy is to use papers that are natural, renewable and recyclable products and made from wood grown in well-managed forests and other controlled sources. The logging and manufacturing processes are expected to conform to the environmental regulations of the country of origin.

Contents

Content Guidance

Questions & Answers

■Getting the most from this book

Exam tips

Advice on key points in the text to help you learn and recall content, avoid pitfalls, and polish your exam technique in order to boost your grade.

Knowledge check

Rapid-fire questions throughout the Content Guidance section to check your understanding. Answers are given at the back of the book.

Key quotation

Useful quotations to help you get to grips with the topics.

Key thinkers

Ensure you are familiar with the key people named in the specification.

Exam-style questions

Commentary on the questions

Tips on what you need to do to gain full marks, indicated by the icon **e**

Sample student answers

Practise the questions, then look at the student answers that follow.

Commentary on sample student answers

Read the comments (preceded by the icon **e**) showing how many marks each answer would be awarded in the exam and exactly where marks are gained or lost.

Questions & Answers

■Question 1: Explore

Question 1

Explore the work of one leading figure in the fight for equality. [8 marks]

e The command word 'Explore' requires you to demonstrate understanding by investigating different reasons, concepts and ideas.

In this question you are being asked to show knowledge and understanding of the views of one leading figure in the fight for equality. You need to choose one from gender, race or disability equality. For example, Martin Luther King is a key figure for race equality and Joni Eareckson Tada is a key figure for disability. You first need to be clear why there is an issue with gender, race or disability equality, and then describe how your chosen figure has helped progress to be made in the fight for equality.

For the AS paper, you should aim to spend 8 minutes. For the A-level paper, you should spend around 10 minutes. You will not have time to write about all the views expressed by your chosen thinker but, in order to achieve level 3, you must show knowledge and understanding of a range of ideas.

Exam tip
'Explore' is both an AS and A-level command word, with questions always worth 8 marks. On the AS exam paper, questions 1 and 4a will use the command word 'Explore'. On the A-level paper it will be question 1 only. This sample question is taken from the A-level only part of the specification.

Student answer A
Martin Luther King advocated affirmative non-violent actions that entailed marches, silent protests and sit-ins to combat racism and segregation in America in the twentieth century. King considered how black people were constantly being discriminated against, leaving many of them unemployed. His famous 'I have a dream' speech, where he argued that he was hopeful for a nation where there would be no more discrimination against black people and where black children would be able to access a good education and good job opportunities, led him to be assassinated. King started off with a small amount of people but soon there were hundreds of people fighting against racism. Many critics argue that his protests were provocative and a threat to the protesters' lives because, while they were not violent, the response from the authorities could be.

e Level 1 awarded.

The focus on Martin Luther King is good but the response is too narrow and general. It needs to develop the context and explain more clearly why there was an issue with inequality, as well as justifying how and why King tried to address it. It also needs development on the Christian element of his thought. The last statement is evaluative and doesn't meet the specific demands of the question.

102 Pearson Edexcel Religious Studies

■About this book

The aim of this guide is to help you prepare for the Pearson Edexcel AS and A-level Religious Studies Paper 2, Religion and ethics. It includes coverage of all of the topics required as part of both the AS examination and the A-level examination. This guide should be used as a supplement for a taught course along with textbooks and other materials recommended by your teacher.

The **Content Guidance** section begins with an introduction to religion and ethics. The rest of the section, split across the six topic areas, summarises the specification content to develop your understanding of the various topics in religion and ethics that will be covered in both the AS examination (Topics 1–3) and the A-level examination (Topics 1–6) of Paper 2, Religion and ethics. Each topic area highlights the works and ideas of key scholars who have made a significant contribution to the understanding of morality and religion. This will prepare you to make a comparison between the works of two named scholars and analyse a specific extract of their work as part of your A-level examination (see below).

The **Questions & Answers** section provides guidance on how to answer both the AS and A-level examination Paper 2. It includes examples of and guidance on the question types you will encounter in the examination. It also includes sample student answers, and examiner comments on how to improve performance.

Specification

For Paper 2, at both AS and A-level, you will be required to:

- explore issues arising in the areas of morality and religion
- study underlying ideas and concepts, and how ethical and religious ideas are applied to contemporary social, political and personal situations
- develop the skills needed for further study through examining specific practical problems such as equality, war and peace, and sexual ethics
- engage with a representative range of ethical stances and the views of significant ethical thinkers

At A-level *only* you will be required to further deepen and extend your understanding of religion and ethics by:

- considering the relevance of language in discussing moral issues
- identifying common ground between religion and morality
- studying key scholars who have made a significant contribution, either historically or in the present, to shaping modern ethical theory
- exploring the links between this paper and other areas of study
- applying ethical theory to medical ethics, in the context of debates about the beginning and end of life

In the A-level examination, it is compulsory for students to compare the work of two named scholars, including a specific extract of their work. These are published in the relevant pages of the *A Level Religious Studies Anthology*, which can be downloaded from the Pearson Edexcel website.

Content Guidance

■ Introduction to religion and ethics

What is ethics?

Ethics is the branch of philosophy which considers and explains moral principles and moral conduct and investigates the meaning of moral language.

Morality understood in an everyday sense broadly means having some kind of system of values — deciding what is right or wrong for yourself. Ethics, however, takes a much more systematic and critical approach to the question. The focus of ethics is indeed the notion of right and wrong, but what it attempts to explain is *why* people make certain moral decisions and *how* we create moral systems which tell us how to act.

Some ethical theories also aim to tell us what moral standards we should choose and how we could achieve the good life. While non-philosophers see morality as a set of rules to obey and principles to follow, moral philosophers go beyond that and seek reasons why we should adopt a certain system of values, and consider the logic behind moral judgement.

Key quotation

Anyone can get angry — that is easy — or give or spend money; but to do this to the right person, to the right extent, at the right time, with the right motive, and in the right way, that is not for everyone, nor is it easy.

Aristotle

Ethical thinking involves thinking critically about what, as a person, you should do, what others should do and what sort of person you should be.

Examples of ethical questions are:
- How ought we to live?
- What makes our actions right or wrong?
- What does it mean to call actions right or wrong?
- Do non-human animals have rights?
- What is the link between religion and morality?

Key quotation

The first step away from being manipulated, and towards a more autonomous outlook, is to stand back from a set of responses and think.

Jonathan Glover

What is a moral issue?

One of the first tasks of moral philosophy is to be clear on what makes an action moral and to differentiate between moral and non-moral judgements. Clearly, it is not a moral judgement to tell a friend that the red coat on display in a shop window would look nice on her, whereas it *is* a moral judgement to tell her that she shouldn't buy a red coat made by child labourers in India. But how can we explain the difference between the two?

The main difference between moral and non-moral issues is that moral issues are based on values rather than facts.

- A fact is a descriptive statement about the world, but could also be what the law says, what religions say or what takes place in nature. For example, the statement that 'people are banned from smoking in public places in the UK' is a fact.
- A value, however, is never intended to be simply descriptive: it is a judgement about the world and implies the acceptance or rejection of norms of behaviour, and the understanding of terms such as 'right' or 'wrong'. For example, the statement that 'people shouldn't smoke in front of their children' implies a value judgement.

Moral philosophers investigate the relationship between facts and values, which means how we view the world and the moral principles we adopt.

Philosophers recognise certain requirements as essential to be able to have moral choice and make moral decisions. A moral agent is a being who is capable of moral decisions, and with this capacity comes responsibility for the moral or immoral behaviour chosen. The main criteria for moral agency are the following:

- We need to be free to make choices — moral philosophers assume we have free will.
- We need to be rational — able to look at the pros and cons of decisions and weigh up consequences.
- We need to be self-aware and conscious — we understand that we are the ones performing the action.
- The act must be intentional.
- The act has an effect on others, in so far as it can benefit them or harm them.

Most of us would agree that non-human animals and very young children are not moral agents. But what about older children and teenagers? Or adults in the early stages of dementia?

The three main approaches to ethics

There are three main types of approach to ethics:

- Ethical theories, also called normative theories, look at how we make and should make moral decisions. They consider how a foundation for moral thinking is provided by the consequences of an action (utilitarianism), our intentions (deontological theories) or the development of character (virtue theory).
- Meta-ethical theories consider the nature and status of ethical language, and question whether the Good is a property of the world or a reflection of our emotions. Moral realism argues that moral truths or facts exist — that when we say 'good', for example, we are referring to an objective property that exists in the world.

> **Key quotation**
>
> Philosophy ought to question the basic assumptions of the age. Thinking through, critically and carefully, what most of us take for granted is, I believe, the chief task of philosophy, and the task that makes philosophy a worthwhile activity.
>
> Peter Singer

Moral anti-realism argues that moral truths do not exist and that moral judgements are simply based on individual likes and dislikes.

■ Applied ethics considers more specific moral dilemmas and problems. Applied or practical ethics is the area which has the most relevance to our everyday life. One of the main aims of applied ethics is to solve moral dilemmas in a systematic and philosophical way.

Each of these approaches tries to explain what we mean by morality and moral terms such as 'good', 'right' and 'wrong', as well as what moral standards we should adopt as we go about our daily lives.

Important thinkers in religion and ethics

The work of a range of philosophers and other thinkers from across the centuries is introduced within the different sections of this book, some writing from within the Christian tradition and others not. You may make reference to them when discussing particular ideas or themes as follows:

■ **Significant concepts in issues or debates in religion and ethics:** James Lovelock, Arne Næss, Martin Luther King, Joni Eareckson Tada

■ **A study of three ethical theories:** Jeremy Bentham, J. S. Mill, J. A. T. Robinson, John Fletcher, Aquinas, Bernard Hoose

■ **Application of ethical theories to issues of importance:** Augustine, Aquinas, Peter Vardy, Jack Dominian

■ **Ethical language:** G. E. Moore, A. J. Ayer, Richard Dawkins, R. A. Sharpe

■ **Deontology, virtue ethics and the works of scholars:** W. D. Ross, Thomas Nagel, Philippa Foot, Alasdair MacIntyre; comparing the writings of Immanuel Kant and Aristotle

■ **Medical ethics: beginning and end of life issues:** Peter Singer, Jonathan Glover

Areas of religion and ethics for study

This book covers a wide range of ideas and issues and identifies a number of areas of religion and ethics on which questions may be set in the examination.

Significant concepts in issues or debates in religion and ethics

The first topic looks at two contemporary areas of debate that have both ethical and religious dimensions:

■ the relationship between humans and their environment — To what extent is the environment ours to use and what is our duty of care towards it?

■ issues of equality — How can we safeguard the rights of everyone and ensure that no one is discriminated against on the grounds of gender, race or physical ability?

A study of three ethical theories

Much of moral philosophy has been concerned with developing systems of normative ethics in order to provide guidance for what people should do and rules to guide action.

This section considers three such theories:

- utilitarianism — a secular ethical theory which argues that the morality of an action is based on its consequences and how much pleasure or happiness it creates
- situation ethics — a liberal Christian theory of ethics which argues that the central concern of ethics should be agape, or selfless love
- natural law theory — a divine command theory which argues that God creates rational moral laws for us to follow and we can work them out using reason

Application of ethical theories to issues of importance

This section covers two important ethical debates:

- just war — Can a war ever be just and morally justifiable? Can there be good reasons to start a war? Can there be moral ways to conduct a war and a moral way to act once it is over?
- sexual ethics — What sexual behaviours can be considered moral or immoral in our liberal society? Do religious approaches still matter or are they outdated?

Ethical language

This section looks at the meaning of ethical terms or meta-ethics and considers:

- moral realist and anti-realist approaches
- the relationship between religion and morality — Is a belief in God necessary to be moral? Do contemporary issues concerning religion undermine the connection between religion and morality?

Deontology, virtue ethics and the works of scholars

This section considers two more ethical theories in the context of the work of Immanuel Kant and Aristotle, respectively:

- deontological ethics — the argument that the morality of an action is based on intentions and motive
- virtue theory — the argument that to be moral is to develop your character and cultivate the virtues necessary to become a good person

Medical ethics: beginning and end of life issues

This final section considers two key areas of medical ethics:

- What is the status of the embryo? What are the ethical debates around procedures such as pre-implantation genetic diagnosis (PGD), use of stem cells and cord blood, *in vitro* fertilisation (IVF), destruction of embryos and abortion?
- Can assisted dying be considered moral? This involves ethical debates about euthanasia, palliative care, current legal positions and concepts of rights and responsibilities, personhood and human nature, options and choices.

The *Anthology*

You will need to refer to an anthology of extracts from four works. There will be questions set on these specific texts, but you should also be able to apply the texts to any area of study within the specification. The texts are as follows:

- Barclay, W. (1971) 'Situation Ethics', Chapter 4 in *Ethics in a Permissive Society*, Collins, pp. 69–91

Exam tip

The specification refers to named scholars in almost all sections and this is reflected in this Student Guide. However, students are not restricted to referring to these thinkers alone and wider reading around the topics is recommended.

- Kant, I. (2002) Second section in *Groundwork for the Metaphysics of Morals*, Yale University Press, pp. 29–47
- Aristotle (1980) 'Moral Virtue', Book II in *The Nicomachean Ethics*, Oxford World's Classics, pp. 23–26
- Wilcockson, M. (1999) 'Euthanasia and Doctors' Ethics', Chapter 4 in *Issues of Life and Death*, Hodder Education, pp. 56–69

The full prescribed texts are available online via the Pearson Edexcel website, https://qualifications.pearson.com.

■ Significant concepts in issues or debates in religion and ethics

Environmental issues

Environmental ethics is an area of philosophy which considers the moral relationship human beings have with the environment and with other animals. People generally agree that we have certain duties and obligations towards the environment but differ as to what those are — and why. Do human beings have responsibilities towards the environment because humans have a special status? Or do they need to make sure the environment is sustainable in order to keep making use of it? Do non-human living beings have intrinsic worth and value regardless of their utility to humans?

A religious perspective: Christianity

Christianity encourages people to care for and protect the environment. This is broadly, what we mean by **environmentalism**. Two central concepts support this:

- **stewardship** — the idea that God has given humanity the task of looking after the Earth
- **conservation** — the idea that humanity should protect natural resources and the environment and maintain them for the future

These concepts are not exclusive to Christianity, but the idea that these responsibilities are God-given arises directly from the Bible.

Stewardship versus dominion

The Book of Genesis describes how human beings are created as the pinnacle of creation. The animals are brought to Adam to be named and this is significant because, in Hebrew thinking, the act of naming gives power over what is named. Genesis says that humans are given 'dominion' over all other species. Humans alone are made in God's image and so they alone represent God on Earth.

Exam tip

Use this link to access the *Anthology*: https://tinyurl.com/yargzcu6

Environmentalism
A concern with the long-term effect of human activities, the survival of species and the health of the environment.

Knowledge check 1

What is environmental ethics and why is it important?

Key quotation

Then God said, 'Let us make man in our image, after our likeness. And let them have dominion over the fish of the sea and over the birds of the heavens and over the livestock and over all the earth and over every creeping thing that creeps on the earth.'
Genesis 1:26

Note on quotations

All quotations from the Bible in this book are from the English Standard Version.

Many Christians believe that humans were created by God in order to care for the rest of creation; this is **stewardship**. Humans have a responsibility to look after God's creation, because they alone have been made in God's image.

However, Christians disagree about the meaning of the word 'dominion'. Some think it means stewardship; others take it to mean 'power over', which has important ethical implications.

The notion of science during the Renaissance and the Enlightenment was very much a philosophy of domination: science and technology could bring benefits to society as a whole. Francis Bacon (1561–1626), for example, argued that nature was a slave and that the purpose of science was to control it.

More modern readings argue that the role God has given human beings is that of carers or stewards. Richard Bauckham (b.1946), a leading biblical scholar and theologian, argues that the opening chapters of Genesis support this view. At every stage of the creation process, God sees that what he has created is good, and when he finishes he sees that the whole of creation is good. That implies that what he has created has value, a value that goes beyond being a means to an end for human consumption. Dominion means responsible stewardship.

There is a strong tradition of love and care for the environment among some of the Christian saints and teachers. St John Chrysostom (347–407) and St Francis of Assisi (1181–1226) both taught that man must love and protect the whole of creation.

St Francis is often portrayed with animals — with birds sitting on his shoulder, pacifying a wolf that had been killing shepherds in a village, preaching to animals. For St Francis, nature was God's creation so being close to creation meant being close to the creator. St Francis's attitude to the world was Christocentric (Christ-centred): since Jesus was God incarnate, Francis took God's appearance within nature as a sign that humans should care for nature as a whole.

Key quotation

The Saints are exceedingly loving and gentle to mankind, and even to brute beasts … surely we ought to show them great kindness and gentleness for many reasons, but, above all, because they are of the same origin as ourselves.
St John Chrysostom

In his *Homilies*, St John Chrysostom expressed a sense of love, compassion and respect for all of God's creation: for people, for animals and for the environment.

Stewardship The idea that human beings have a special place in the natural world and have an essential responsibility for it. Christians would regard this responsibility as God-given.

Key quotation

If you have men who will exclude any of God's creatures from the shelter of compassion and pity, you will have men who will deal likewise with their fellow men.
St Francis of Assisi

Modern ethical implications of stewardship

While the Bible is in one sense a historical text, its message still has relevance to human beings today. Stewardship has become an important concept in Christian environmental ethics:

- Evangelical churches often strongly support the view that Christians must care for the environment. The Evangelical Environmental Network refers to 'creation-care', that is, preventing activities that harm God's creation and helping human beings become better stewards.
- The Church of England states that God has entrusted the world to humankind and therefore we are responsible for it; we are the Earth's curators and trustees. Stewardship is about caring management, not selfish exploitation.
- The Catholic Church's position starts with an understanding of human beings in relation to God. Human beings are created in the image of God; that implies that humankind has a similar role to play. Just as God maintains the universe, the role of humankind is to maintain God's creation, which means to be responsible for it and take care of it.

Conservation

Although by no means a solely Christian movement, conservationism is an approach to the environment that many Christians take because of the central idea of stewardship. Conservation refers to the protection of natural resources and the environment from the dangers of climate change and human activities like deforestation, over-fishing and industry with polluting effects. It encompasses the ethics of how to allocate, protect and use resources (including other species) responsibly and regulate human use of oceans, forests and so on.

Conserving the environment is necessary to protect future generations of animals but also future generations of humanity. The concept of conservation is thus tightly linked to Christian arguments for stewardship.

Challenges to the Christian approach

In a lecture given in 1967, later published in *Science*, the professor of medieval history Lynn Townsend White (1907–87) argued controversially that Christianity was to blame for the environmental crisis we are facing today. In his article, 'The Historical Roots of our Ecological Crisis', he argues that the Bible asserts man's dominion over nature and establishes an anthropocentric world-view that sees other life forms as subservient to humanity. Furthermore, the distinction between man as made in God's image and the rest of creation implies that other creatures are soulless and therefore inferior.

Key quotation

Man named all the animals, thus establishing his dominance over them. God planned all of this explicitly for man's benefit and rule: no item in the physical creation had any purpose save to serve man's purposes. And, although man's body is made of clay, he is not simply part of nature: he is made in God's image.

Lynn Townsend White

Conservation The act of creating the circumstances necessary to preserve and protect species and ecosystems.

Anthropocentric Centred on humanity.

Knowledge check 2

What is the difference between dominion and stewardship?

For White, Christianity is ultimately responsible for climate change, global warming, deforestation and so on because it fundamentally supports the exploitation of the natural world for man's benefit.

White doesn't suggest that a secular approach is necessarily better, rather that Christian guilt over the destruction of the environment should push Christians to change their world-view and adapt religious views to the current crisis. Religion still has a role to play as it helps us understand our place in the world and our role in sustaining it. Christianity and ecology are compatible.

Not all denominations support environmentalism

Not all Christian denominations support environmentalism. Early Christians placed eschatological beliefs before any other considerations. These Christians believed that our existence on Earth was only temporary and that the end of the world would lead to resurrection.

Some evangelical Christians argue that our real life starts in heaven and that since the old Earth will be replaced by a new one, there is no purpose to protection and conservation. Some go as far as saying that the current environmental crisis is a sign of the end and that Earth will soon be destroyed. Mass deaths of animals are considered by such groups as eschatological signs — signs of the end of the world.

Some groups argue that the Earth is temporary and can therefore be used for profitable purposes. Others, however, argue for transformation rather than destruction. The Earth will be transformed and renewed, and that is why we have a duty of care.

The Cornwall Alliance

Ronald Nash (1936–2006) and the Cornwall Alliance have been prominent critics of environmentalism, which they call the Green Dragon. They are very critical of the ideological link between some evangelical churches and supposedly 'extremist' environmental groups such as Greenpeace and Earth First.

The Cornwall Alliance understands stewardship as a God-given duty to be responsible for the natural world but disagrees with the social movement that is environmentalism and its argument that we have a duty to protect entire species and ecosystems. It is critical of environmentalist policies to fight global warming which, in its view, waste money and prevent poor countries from using the fossil fuels they need to rise out of poverty, and so effectively perpetuate the cycle of hunger, disease and death. Political leaders should implement policies which defend the rights and liberties of individuals and make energy more affordable.

The Cornwall Alliance is particularly critical of what it regards as radical environmentalism — the argument that all living beings have intrinsic value. It blames the influence of deep ecology on Christian environmentalism: the view that nature is created by God and human beings have a moral duty to be good stewards. Nature is not God. The view that God is everywhere in nature is a form of pantheism, which for Nash is fundamentally anti-Christian. He is also critical of pantheist tendencies to see human beings as having no more value than any other living creature, which is the deep ecology argument. The alliance argues for a stewardship of creation which is not radical and which is apolitical.

Secular Unconnected with or independent of religion.

Eschatological Relating to the afterlife.

Key quotation

Then I saw a new heaven and a new earth, for the first heaven and the first earth had passed away, and the sea was no more.

Revelation 21:1

Pantheism The view that God is everywhere in nature.

Secular approaches to environmental ethics

Deep ecology

Deep ecology, advocated by Arne Næss in particular, is a secular position that claims to be supported by both science and philosophy. Although it is a secular movement, it has a strong spiritual element.

> **Deep ecology** A belief that human and non-human species are equal and integral elements of the global ecosystem.

Key thinker

Arne Næss (1912–2009)

Arne Næss was a Norwegian philosopher and mountaineer who founded the deep ecology movement, inspired by Rachel Carson's 1962 book *Silent Spring*. He argued that all life has value, not just human life, and that the natural world has inherent worth, independent of its usefulness to humans. He promoted non-violent Gandhian direct action as a central tenet of the movement.

Næss argued that nature has intrinsic value regardless of its utility to human beings and was critical of Christian anthropocentrism. All living beings should be able to flourish and evolve naturally. Environmentalism should not just be about conservation and sustainability but about a consideration of the worth of nature and ecosystems. Human beings have a moral obligation to protect the environment.

The spiritual element of deep ecology comes from Næss's personal connection with nature. He saw nature as sacred and felt the need to live in harmony with it. He argued that we need to:

- radically reduce Earth's population
- abandon all goals of economic growth
- conserve diversity of species
- live in small, self-reliant communities
- minimise our impact on the environment

Næss called this 'ecosophy'. Our approach to the environment must move away from an anthropocentric ideology towards a more holistic (meaning 'whole') approach which values the intrinsic worth of nature and the environment. Shallow ecology (which encompasses recycling, sustainability and conservation programmes) is necessary but is not sufficient.

Deep ecology has its critics. The Cornwall Alliance argues that it leads to pantheism. The American philosopher Anthony Weston (b.1954) argues that the main focus of environmentalism should be technological solutions and ecological change. He is very critical of deep ecology's focus on universal principle and instead thinks institutions and practices need to change from the bottom up.

Shallow ecology

Shallow ecology is a theory of environmental ethics which mostly focuses on conservation. It values the environment but doesn't give it intrinsic worth as the deep ecology movement does; instead, the natural world has instrumental value as a means to an end. For example, it would argue as follows:

- Biodiversity needs to be sustained because plants can provide essential medicines.
- The rainforest should be preserved on the basis of its utility as the Earth's lungs.

- We should aim to prevent the extinction of species, but only if it is of value to human beings.

The problem with such an approach is that it doesn't take into account the value we give to nature and the environment. People enjoy spending time in the natural world and admire its beauty; they watch animals in the wild, swim with dolphins — all this in recognition of the fact that we have moral responsibilities towards the natural world simply because it has worth beyond the uses we ascribe to it.

The Gaia hypothesis and eco-holism

James Lovelock created the Gaia hypothesis in the 1960s and published his thesis in 1979. *Gaia* is a Greek term for the Earth goddess. Lovelock coined the term to symbolise Earth as a sustaining and nurturing system.

> **Key thinker**
>
> ### James Lovelock (b.1919)
> Lovelock is a British independent scientist, doctor, author and environmentalist whose Gaia hypothesis argues that the Earth is a self-regulating super-organism. A former designer at NASA, he is also known for inventing the electron capture detector. With it, he became one of the first people to detect CFCs — chlorofluorocarbons, implicated in the greenhouse effect — in the atmosphere.

Lovelock sees the Earth as a single living entity, a kind of super-organism. Living beings and non-living entities are interdependent; the relationship between organic and non-organic entities is truly symbiotic (i.e. beneficial to both parties).

Like a living being, the Earth has a self-regulating mechanism. There is an internal balance between the following:
- the biosphere (ecological systems)
- the atmosphere (the layer of gases surrounding Earth)
- the hydrosphere (the liquid component of Earth)
- the lithosphere (the outer section of Earth and its crust)

The inner workings of Gaia, therefore, can be viewed as a study of the physiology of the Earth, where the oceans and rivers are its blood, the atmosphere its lungs, the land its bones, and the living organisms its senses.

The conditions for life are precisely defined, so very small fluctuations in any of the parameters could be catastrophic for life on Earth. This is what is happening with CO_2 emissions: the system is no longer able to cope with them and maintain itself in a way that can sustain human life. Life would not necessarily be destroyed by changes to the environment: the fossil record shows us that. Human life may be wiped out, but humans are just part of Gaia; Gaia herself would survive. If we abuse Gaia we risk our own survival. Gaia owes us nothing but we owe her our very existence.

Lovelock argues for eco-holism, a focus on the interdependence of the whole ecosystem. Like Næss, Lovelock challenges the view that humans are the most important species. We shouldn't be anthropocentric but rather should be biocentric and allow Gaia to restore balance after the imbalance caused by humans.

Knowledge check 3

Explain the difference between deep and shallow ecology.

Key quotation

There aren't just bad people that commit genocide; we are all capable of it. It's our evolutionary history.

James Lovelock

Eco-holism An environmental movement which views all biotic (living) and abiotic components of the ecosystem as interdependent and having inherent worth.

Animal welfare and protection

Those who, like Aquinas and Descartes, believe that animals do not have souls arguably have a ready-made argument for not worrying too much about pain inflicted on animals through factory farming and animal experimentation. However, most people would argue that we still have a duty of care and an obligation to prevent unnecessary suffering.

The concepts of dominion and stewardship assume a right for humans to control the environment. If it becomes a matter of preserving the human species or another species, then the human good and benefit will inevitably come first. Some of the main arguments for this view are:

- Humans in the world are starving.
- Humans are more important than animals.
- Humans are objects of moral concern whereas animals are not part of the moral community.
- There are no situations in which the death of a human is less important than the death of an animal.

Peter Singer on animal welfare

Key thinker

Peter Singer (b.1946)
The Australian moral philosopher Peter Singer is professor of bioethics at Princeton University. He is best known for his defence of animal rights, including his 1975 book *Animal Liberation*, and for his philosophy of preference utilitarianism. He has also written about global poverty and founded the organisation The Life You Can Save.

Singer insists that animals have intrinsic value. Like the founder of utilitarianism, Jeremy Bentham, Singer's sole criterion as to whether or not an animal can be an object of moral concern is its ability to feel pain and pleasure. All pet owners and farmers know that animals can feel pain and pleasure — even though they don't express it as we do — and therefore they are objects of moral concern. According to this view, the environments of all species that can feel pain and pleasure should be protected.

Singer argues that since we do not kill or eat or experiment on babies, or adults in a coma, we should extend the same respect to animals. If we have a responsibility to weaker humans, we have a responsibility to animals also. Singer argues against the view that human beings have more rights than animals on the grounds that humans are rational and have free will, language and so on. For him, this view is a prejudice akin to racism, which he calls **speciesism**.

Some Christian views

Some Christians take the view that environmental protection must be for the benefit of the environment as a whole. They regard the environment as having intrinsic value, so its protection should be an end in itself.

Key quotation

All the arguments to prove man's superiority cannot shatter this hard fact: in suffering the animals are our equals.

Peter Singer

Speciesism The assumption that human beings are the superior species.

Religious people who subscribe to environmental approaches such as deep ecology and the Gaia hypothesis take the same line, but for an additional reason: if the environment as a whole does not benefit, then humans will not benefit either. Environmental protection must be aimed at the biosphere, and not at any single part of it. The need for environmental protection is a direct result of human technological development which has harnessed other species, both sentient and otherwise. So, in terms of simple fairness, environmental protection ought to be for the good of all species that are affected, sentient or otherwise.

Humans share 99% of their genes with apes and evolved from a common ancestor. Religious resistance to the theory of evolution has tended to blur the fact that in protecting animals, we are protecting our own kind.

Christians appeal to the Sanctity of Life Principle (SOLP) (meaning 'life is sacred') in order to decide what to do in a number of situations in which the correct moral action is a matter of debate. For example, the principle is used by most Christians to forbid euthanasia: if life is sacred, then it ought not to be removed.

The SOLP derives from Genesis 1:26–7: humans were made in God's image, from which many conclude that human life must therefore be sacred or holy. Some Christians extend this principle to all life forms: if God created life, and if Jesus as God is immanent within nature, then surely all life is sacred. Environmental protection should therefore be for all life.

Key quotation

Human babies are not born self-aware, or capable of grasping that they exist over time. They are not persons … The life of a newborn is of less value than the life of a pig, a dog, or a chimpanzee.

Peter Singer

Knowledge check 4

Why, according to Singer, are animals objects of moral concern?

Environmental issues: summary

- Environmental ethics refer to the moral and/or religious duties human beings have towards the environment.
- The Christian argument of stewardship states that we have a duty of care towards the natural world, a responsibility given to us by God.
- The Christian argument that humans have dominion over the Earth implies that the environment has no intrinsic value other than as a resource for humanity.
- The Cornwall Alliance argues for stewardship but is against environmentalism.
- Not all churches support stewardship because of eschatological considerations.
- The secular approach of deep ecology views nature as having intrinsic value and rejects an anthropocentric view of the environment. All living beings on Earth have a right to live.

- The secular approach of shallow ecology is anthropocentric: the natural world has no intrinsic value but must be conserved to give human beings a sustainable future.
- Eco-holism based on Lovelock's Gaia hypothesis argues that the Earth is a holistic biosphere in which every entity is interdependent and in which the human race is of no particular significance in the long run.
- While Christians argue that we have dominion over animals or that we have a duty of care as stewardship, both views assume that human beings have more value than animals. Human beings are created in the image of God, animals are not.
- Peter Singer is very critical of this speciesist view and argues instead for the moral rights of every single species.

Equality

Equality is one of the core values of Western societies, alongside individual freedom. In the UK, the Equality Act 2010 merges over 116 pieces of anti-discrimination legislation, including the Sexual Discrimination Act 1975, the Race Relations Act 1976 and the Disability Discrimination Act 1995.

Equality doesn't mean treating everybody in exactly the same way; rather, it means treating everyone fairly. Unfortunately, legislation alone cannot guarantee fair treatment and equality of opportunity in practice.

Equality itself is a contested concept and can mean different things — political, moral or religious equality, for example. Politicians also talk a lot about equality of opportunity versus equality of outcome.

Christianity and gender equality

Even up to the present day, religions such as Christianity have stood accused of misogyny and of condoning prejudice, discrimination and even abuse of women.

While Christians believe that we are all made in the image of God and that God loves us equally, certain passages in the Bible appear to suggest that women are inferior to men.

What does the Bible say?

- In Genesis, God creates Eve by taking one of Adam's ribs. She is his companion and they have to take care of the Garden of Eden together. But it is Eve who gives in to temptation. God punishes her and states that her husband will rule over her.
- The stories in the Bible reveal a patriarchal society. Men could divorce their wives, but women could not divorce their husbands. Women were seen as unclean while they were menstruating or after the birth of a child. God is referred to as 'He', as God the Father and so on. Jesus has no female disciples. Mary, the mother of Jesus, and Mary Magdalene, a prostitute who redeemed herself and became his follower, had important but essentially domestic and supportive roles.
- St Paul is often seen as a misogynistic figure. Paul's writings have influenced the growth and development of the Christian Church since the first century. Some passages from his Epistles seem to support the view that women are subordinate and inferior to men.

Key quotations

Wives, submit to your own husbands, as to the Lord. For the husband is the head of the wife even as Christ is the head of the church, his body, and is himself its Saviour.

Ephesians 5:22–3

Let a woman learn quietly with all submissiveness. I do not permit a woman to teach or to exercise authority over a man; rather, she is to remain quiet.

1 Timothy 2:11–12

Historically, the Christian Church has upheld the norms of a patriarchal society. The Protestant reformer Martin Luther (1483–1546), for example, argued that the role of women is to stay at home, take care of the house and have children. The Catholic

Exam tip

In the exam you will only be expected to write about one area of equality — gender equality, racial equality or disability rights. You will need to know about one significant figure in your chosen area and consider both a religious and a secular perspective.

Equality of opportunity Equal chance of advancement for all.

Equality of outcome Equality of material wealth.

Misogyny Hating or fearing women.

Church still condemns abortion and the use of artificial contraception, effectively denying Catholic women rights over their own reproduction available to other women. The first women priests were not ordained in the Church of England until 1994 and the first woman bishop wasn't officially consecrated until 2015.

Fundamentally, though, the Christian religion views women as equal to men. While men and women have different gender roles, they are equal in the eyes of God. God himself has many supposedly 'feminine' qualities: God heals, feeds, comforts, remembers and forgives.

Many Old Testament women have significant roles: Esther saved the Jews from death; Ruth set an example of love and loyalty; Deborah was a prophet whose wisdom was much admired.

In the New Testament, Jesus's treatment of women was revolutionary for his time. Jesus preached in the Jerusalem temple, in the court of the women, and on another occasion talked freely with a racially mixed Samaritan woman who had broken social taboos by having five husbands. Jesus also showed supposedly 'feminine' qualities — love, tenderness, gentleness, compassion — and cried openly after the death of Lazarus. Some of his closest followers were women; indeed, 'after the resurrection Jesus appeared first to women' (Matthew 28:1–10).

Modern Christian attitudes

Some Christians argue that men and women should be treated the same in every way because both men and women are created in the image of God. This equal treatment should include positions of responsibility within the Church to reflect wider social change.

Others believe that men and women are equally valuable to God, but have different qualities — physical, psychological and emotional. Their different gifts should be put to different uses. The argument is that Jesus did not choose men to be his apostles by accident and some roles in the Church are more suitable for men.

Attitudes to women priests

The United Reformed Church and the Salvation Army have always had women ministers. The Baptist Church has had women ministers since the 1920s. The ordination of the first female Church of England vicars in 1994 caused widespread division, and some male leaders, as well as other men and women, left the Church in protest.

The Roman Catholic and Orthodox churches do not allow women priests. This is because Jesus chose men to be his apostles and the foundation of the Church, not women. Jesus's authority has also been passed on through men. When celebrating the Eucharist, the priest represents Christ, who was a man. Women cannot play this role.

Secular attitudes to gender equality

Classic liberal ideology argues for fundamental equal rights for both men and women, and for freedom of speech and action. This view is often associated with the British philosophers John Locke (1632–1704) and John Stuart Mill.

Key quotation

As one whom his mother comforts, so I will comfort you; you shall be comforted in Jerusalem.

Isaiah 66:13

J. S. Mill on women

In *On Liberty*, Mill argues that people should be free to do what they want, as long as they do not harm others — the harm principle.

In *The Subjection of Women*, published in 1869, Mill put forward an argument for political and social equality between men and women at a time when women in Britain had very few rights. Equality laws are very much the outcome of such philosophical positions, combined with the activism of generations of women who have fought and defended their right to vote, work and have control over their own bodies. Liberal views of the role of women can at times be at odds with religious views in that liberal thinkers reject the traditional domestic role of women, or at the very least argue that the female gender is compatible with positions of leadership and responsibility in all areas of society.

Elizabeth Cady Stanton

Elizabeth Cady Stanton (1815–1902) was an American women's rights campaigner who was deeply inspired by Mill and other liberal philosophers. Stanton was very critical of the Christian churches' attitudes to women and saw them as key contributors to women's oppression. In 1895–98, she published *The Woman's Bible*, a series of essays discussing the scriptural treatment of women and why that needed to change.

Stanton was advocating for women's rights at the time of the abolitionist movement, when the USA was preparing to amend the Constitution to outlaw slavery and give black men the right to vote. She became concerned that the issue of women's rights was being sidelined by abolitionist activities, and her speeches demonstrate racist views and advocate the vote for educated white middle-class men and women only.

Christianity and racism

Racism can take a number of forms:

- direct racism — where someone is treated differently, less favourably, or not given the same opportunities as others because of their ethnicity or skin colour
- indirect racism — where certain practices, policies or rules disadvantage a particular community or section of society, for example the banning of headscarves
- institutional racism — racism present within social institutions, such as governmental organisations, police forces or the army

While Christianity teaches that everyone is equal in the eyes of God, the history of Christianity and certain passages of the Bible suggest that the Christian message may not be so clear-cut.

Is the Bible racist?

Most Christians would argue that the Bible is not racist, because racism goes against the fundamental Christian value that we are created equal and loved equally by God. However, slavery is arguably the most catastrophic form of discrimination yet there is no explicit condemnation of slavery in the Bible. Indeed, some Old Testament passages appear to condone slavery.

Key quotations

When a man strikes his slave, male or female, with a rod and the slave dies under his hand, he shall be avenged. But if the slave survives a day or two, he is not to be avenged, for the slave is his money.

Exodus 21:20–21

Bondservants, obey your earthly masters with fear and trembling, with a sincere heart, as you would Christ, not by the way of eye-service, as people-pleasers, but as bondservants of Christ, doing the will of God from the heart.

Ephesians 6:5–6

Likewise, in the New Testament, Jesus seems tacitly to accept the practice. Although Jesus uses slavery as an analogy, to make people understand our relationship with God, he doesn't openly condemn slavery as a social practice when he condemns other traditional practices and the shunning of some communities.

The Bible is a historical document and slavery was common and widely accepted at that time. However, those who wrote the various books of the Bible claimed to be divinely inspired. Can God be all-loving if he implicitly condones a practice in which not all human beings are treated equally? If there is no conflict between Christian faith and slave-owning, is there likewise no conflict between being a Christian and discriminating on the basis of race or ethnicity?

On the other hand, certain Old Testament passages make explicit reference to a duty to treat 'foreigners' as you would your own people. Passages from the New Testament also suggest that prejudice and discrimination are wrong and that the Church should concentrate on unity, one of Jesus's main messages.

Key quotations

You shall treat the stranger who sojourns with you as the native among you, and you shall love him as yourself, for you were strangers in the land of Egypt: I am the Lord your God.

Leviticus 19:34

There is neither Jew nor Greek, there is neither slave nor free, there is no male and female, for you are all one in Christ Jesus.

St Paul, Galatians 3:28

Church responses to racism

While the history of Christianity is littered with stories of discrimination, abuse and racism perpetuated in the name of religion, we can equally find examples of Christians fighting for the abolition of slavery or saving their Jewish neighbours from the Nazis, of Christian missionaries fighting for the rights of ethnic minorities, and so forth. Christian churches have now embraced equality in their policies and procedures. All UK Christian churches agree that racism and discrimination have no place in Christianity and the Church was involved in bringing about the Race Relations Act.

The Roman Catholic Church has a long history of fighting racism, slavery in particular. In 1537 Pope Paul III said keeping a black person as a slave merited excommunication. In 1888 Pope Leo XIII outlawed the slave trade in his letter *In Plurimis*. In the 1980s and 1990s, Pope John Paul II condemned the fact that Christians contributed to the slave trade and argued for the abolition of apartheid in South Africa.

Quakers too have a long history of condemning racism. In the eighteenth century, slave owners or slave traders were not allowed to become Quakers and Quakers were prominent in the abolition movement.

Martin Luther King

Key thinker

Martin Luther King (1929–68)

Baptist minister Martin Luther King became president of the Montgomery Improvement Association in Alabama in 1955. King campaigned tirelessly for civil rights despite many threats to his life. His home was bombed, he was stabbed and his family received death threats. King maintained a commitment to non-violent action throughout. In 1964 he was awarded the Nobel Peace Prize. On 4 April 1968, aged 39, King was shot dead leaving his hotel room.

Although slavery had been abolished in 1869, most black people in the southern states of the USA lived in poverty and had very limited opportunities. On average they earned half the amount white people earned, many could not vote, and segregation in public places — including schools — was common. From 1890, segregation was gradually legalised in the southern states by the Jim Crow laws; legal segregation continued until 1965.

In Montgomery, Alabama, black people had to sit at the back of buses and give up their seat to a white person if requested to do so. On 1 December 1955, Rosa Parks, a middle-aged African-American woman, refused to give up her seat and was arrested. Her act of civil disobedience effectively started the civil rights movement. A black boycott of public buses in Montgomery began on the day of Parks' court hearing and lasted 381 days. The state government eventually passed a law making segregation on buses illegal.

Key quotation

Injustice anywhere is a threat to justice everywhere.

Martin Luther King

Martin Luther King felt strongly that God had created all people as equal and that all people were created in God's image and likeness, as stated in Genesis. At a time when the ordained clergy were focusing on saving souls and remaining apolitical, King felt that it was his Christian duty to help communities have better life chances and achieve equality for all.

King's belief in non-violent direct action was inspired both by his Christian beliefs and by the example of the Indian independence campaigner Mahatma Gandhi. King constantly stressed the need to love your enemies and pray for those who persecuted you (Matthew 5:43–8); violence and hatred could only be conquered by love and forgiveness.

Affirmative non-violent action looked to resist evil and to create understanding and friendship between people and communities — to defeat injustice, not people. King's non-violent protests included sit-ins, freedom marches and silent protests. Non-violent action meant accepting suffering without retaliation, becoming selfless. King argued that suffering can be redemptive and allow us to grow spiritually. King's critics argued that King's non-violent direct action was at times deliberately provocative and put protesters' lives at risk.

Secular responses to racism

Secular responses to racism are, as with gender equality, the outcome of liberal and democratic policies as well as social change. Independent charities like the Runnymede Trust argue that government policies do not do enough to tackle discrimination. The Trust looks particularly at life chances for black and minority ethnic communities, who are still very much under-represented in key institutions such as elite universities, the police, the armed forces and government.

What happens, however, when religious or cultural practices clash with liberal values? For example, female genital mutilation (FGM) is a cultural practice performed in the UK and abroad by people from a variety of religious backgrounds, and involves the partial or complete removal of external female genitalia for non-medical reasons. It is mostly carried out — without anaesthetic — on girls between infancy and age 15. FGM has no health benefits and often results in lifelong health problems, increased risk during childbirth and psychological trauma; it can even lead to death. While liberalism argues for religious and cultural tolerance, it cannot condone practices that lead to inequality. This is why FGM is illegal in the UK.

Christianity and disability

Passages from Leviticus seem to show God discriminating against people with disabilities; they suggest that disabled people are not like 'other people', that they have a different status, that they cannot be close to God and cannot be priests. Consider the following passage:

> And the Lord spoke to Moses, saying, 'Speak to Aaron, saying, None of your offspring throughout their generations who has a blemish may approach to offer the bread of his God. For no one who has a blemish shall draw near, a man blind or lame, or one who has a mutilated face or a limb too long, or a man who has an injured foot or an injured hand, or a hunchback or a dwarf or a man with a defect in his sight or an itching disease or scabs or crushed testicles.'

Key quotation

Nonviolent direct action seeks to create such a crisis and foster such a tension that a community which has constantly refused to negotiate is forced to confront the issue. It seeks so to dramatize the issue that it can no longer be ignored.

Martin Luther King, Birmingham Jail, 1963

Knowledge check 6

Give an example of how Christianity has contributed to greater race equality.

This is a shocking statement but should be understood in relation to the moral values of the time. For the populations that this was written for, disability was understood as a curse or a punishment from God, a sign of impurity. To us, this is clearly wrong, so we now interpret it symbolically. In a symbolic interpretation, the people mentioned are impure because they lack the required virtues to be close to God. Their disabilities are not physical disabilities but weakness of will, poor character. These are the people who cannot worship God.

A significant Old Testament stories is that of Mephibosheth (2 Samuel 9). He was the son of Jonathan, a friend of David, who became king of Israel. Mephibosheth was the only offspring left in the house of Saul, his grandfather and the old king. Mephibosheth could not walk. The tradition of the time would have called for David to kill Mephibosheth, because of his ancestry, but instead David treated Mephibosheth as an honoured guest and gave him his protection and all the property that had belonged to his grandfather. He treated him as an equal.

Corinthians shows that human beings are not created the same, in that humans have different abilities, both physical and intellectual, which are God-given:

> For consider your calling, brothers: not many of you were wise according to worldly standards, not many were powerful, not many were of noble birth. But God chose what is foolish in the world to shame the wise; God chose what is weak in the world to shame the strong; God chose what is low and despised in the world, even things that are not, to bring to nothing things that are, so that no human being might boast in the presence of God.

The Book of Genesis makes it clear that we are all created in the image of God. God is a loving God and forgives our sins. This raises the question as to why some people suffer more, for example through illness and disability. Suffering seems unjust and unbalanced.

The soul-making **theodicy** of the philosopher John Hick argues that suffering allows us to grow spiritually and morally. More importantly, it allows us to close the **epistemic distance** between us and God, to be closer to God. Disability is not a curse, an affliction or a punishment but, for Christians, a way to achieve grace. God does not cause illness or disability but allows it to happen. People with disabilities are equally loved by God.

Jesus didn't shy away from people with disability and didn't exclude them from the faith:

- In Luke 8:43–8 a woman in a crowd touches Jesus's cloak and falls at his feet; she has been bleeding for 12 years and he instantly heals her, telling her that it is her faith that has healed her.
- In Luke 5:11–13 Jesus cures a man with leprosy by touching him. Leprosy was then believed to be a very contagious and dangerous disease, and sufferers were considered untouchable.

Jesus's approach was what we would now call inclusive: he included infectious people, disabled people, adulterers, social outcasts, foreigners and women. In the Sermon on the Mount he declares blessed those whom society considers cursed.

Key quotation

You shall not curse the deaf or put a stumbling block before the blind, but you shall fear your God: I am the Lord.

Leviticus 19:14

Theodicy An argument that seeks to make the existence of evil compatible with the existence of an omnipotent, omnibenevolent God.

Epistemic distance A distance of knowledge, dimension or awareness between humans and God.

Joni Eareckson Tada

Joni Eareckson Tada sees her condition as a gift that has allowed her to do things she would never have done before: painting (she uses her mouth), attaining extensive knowledge of the Bible and setting up her disability charity. She argues that suffering has value and that disabled people are not dependent but interdependent with their families and communities. Rather than looking for miraculous recoveries and divine interventions, we should look at suffering from the point of view that it transforms us. She also understands suffering as the result of sin — that of humankind who has not yet fully embraced Christianity.

Key thinker

Joni Eareckson Tada (b.1949)

Joni Eareckson Tada is a Christian disability activist who argues that suffering has value in the Christian life. Joni became quadriplegic after a diving accident at the age of 17. After years of rehabilitation, religious doubt and struggle, in 1976 she published her autobiography, *Joni*. An international best-seller, the book launched her career as a speaker and activist for the disabled and the voiceless. She is an international advocate for people with disabilities and is the founder and CEO of Joni and Friends International Disability Center in California, which promotes the rights of disabled people and gives support to families.

Key quotation

He has chosen not to heal me, but to hold me. The more intense the pain, the closer His embrace.

Joni Eareckson Tada

Roman Catholicism and disability

Catholic thinking on disability has traditionally been associated with prayer, pilgrimage and miraculous cures. The small French town of Lourdes is famous for the healing power of its sacred spring, for example, while pilgrims to the Vatican in Rome hope that seeing or touching the Pope during mass will cure them.

For many modern Christians, pilgrimage offers as much a psychological healing as a physical one, an opportunity to feel closer to God. These sacred places are not just for people with an illness or disability, but for every Roman Catholic. Moreover, attitudes to disability in Roman Catholicism are changing. People with a disability are now seen as offering as much to the Church as able-bodied people.

Secular approaches to disability

People with disabilities suffer from discrimination and stereotyping. Compared with non-disabled people, disabled people are more likely to be economically inactive and more likely to experience hate crime or harassment. Medical management of disability has also meant that disabled people with long-term needs become medical cases whose lives revolve around care and treatment, instead of freedom and dignity.

According to the Union of the Physically Impaired Against Segregation (UPIAS), disability is not in the impairment a person experiences but in the social exclusion they experience because of their impairment.

Secular approaches to disability have chiefly been based on the government's equality and diversity policies. The Equality Act 2000 encompasses the Disability Discrimination Act (DDA) 1995. The Act protects people with disability against direct and indirect discrimination, victimisation and harassment. This includes the failure of an organisation to make reasonable adjustment to allow people with disabilities access to goods, facilities, services and employment.

Equality: summary

- In the context of ethics, equality means that people are equal: no one has more rights than anyone else and no one should be discriminated against (directly or indirectly), victimised or harassed.
- In the UK, legislation on gender equality, racial equality, disability rights and so on now falls under the Equality Act 2010.
- Secular approaches focus on making sure that everyone has opportunities and that no one is discriminated against. This stems from liberal principles which place value on human rights and essential freedoms.
- Christian thinking is more complex because certain passages of the Bible suggest that we

are not all equal. However, Christianity promotes a message of love and acceptance and Jesus's preaching reinforces this viewpoint.
- The Christian churches have become more liberal in their understanding of the role of women and, thanks in part to campaigners like Joni Eareckson Tada, increasingly value disabled people as full members of the religious community rather than as members needing support.
- Similarly, churches have worked hard to get rid of racist views within their ranks, especially since the civil rights movements and the actions of Martin Luther King.

■ A study of three ethical theories

Utilitarianism

Consequentialism is the idea that the moral value of an action lies in its consequences. An action is judged to be good when it brings about beneficial consequences, irrespective of the intention behind it. Utilitarianism argues that what is 'good' is the promotion of pleasure or happiness (classical utilitarianism) or of people's preferences (modern utilitarianism).

Consequentialism The view that the moral value of an action lies in its consequences.

Bentham's classical utilitarianism

The classical account of utilitarianism was created by Jeremy Bentham and John Stuart Mill.

Key thinker

Jeremy Bentham (1748–1832)
Bentham was an English philosopher and social reformer. Bentham felt that the English legal system was far too complex and dogmatic. He wanted to create a moral theory which would allow for social and political reforms based on one fundamental rule or axiom. Inspired by the British philosopher Thomas Hobbes (1588–1679), who argued that human beings are fundamentally self-interested, Bentham set out his principle of utility in *An Introduction to the Principles of Morals and Legislation* in 1789.

Classical utilitarianism argues that the ultimate good is pleasure or happiness and is a form of **act utilitarianism**. Human behaviour can be explained by psychological hedonism: pleasure is the sole good and pain the sole evil. The rightness of an action depends entirely on the amount of pleasure it tends to produce.

Key quotation

Nature has placed mankind under the governance of two sovereign masters, pain and pleasure. It is for them alone to point out what we ought to do as well as to determine what we shall do. On the one hand, the standard of right and wrong, on the other, the chain of causes and effects, are fastened to their throne.

Jeremy Bentham

The principle of utility

The principle of utility is that an action ought to be performed only if it brings about the maximum possible happiness for those parties affected by the action: 'the greatest happiness for the greatest number'.

This is, essentially, act utilitarianism — we tally the consequences of each action we perform, and determine on a case-by-case basis whether an action is morally right or wrong. For example, we might need to consider whether an immediate action is going to bring about better consequences than an action in the future. Similarly, if there is a choice between less happiness for the individual but greater net happiness for the community as a whole, the utilitarian must choose the latter.

Key quotation

An action then may be said to be conformable to the principle of utility, or, for shortness sake, to utility (meaning with respect to the community at large), when the tendency it has to augment the happiness of the community is greater than any it has to diminish it.

Jeremy Bentham

The hedonic calculus

Bentham assumed that pleasure and pain were measurable and created a hedonic calculus. This sets out seven criteria by which an individual can measure the pleasure/pain outcome:

1 Intensity — how intense is the pleasure/pain?
2 Duration — how long will the effect last?
3 Certainty/uncertainty — how certain can we be of the outcome of the action?
4 Propinquity/remoteness — is it an action that will affect me or others soon or later in time?
5 Fecundity — will that pleasure/pain produce other pleasures/pains?
6 Purity — how likely is it that the pleasure/pain won't be followed by a sensation of the opposite kind (i.e. pain/pleasure)?
7 Extent — the number of people affected by the act.

Act utilitarianism The view that the rightness of an action is based on the act itself and its consequences in a specific situation.

Knowledge check 7

What does the word 'hedonism' mean?

Knowledge check 8

What is the utilitarian's view of human nature?

For each possibility, you add up all of the pleasure/pain, and then you do whichever action leads to the most pleasure/least pain.

Bentham felt it was important to reduce pain first and then look at pleasure. However, if one course of action involves a small amount of pain but a huge amount of pleasure, it will be better than an action that leads to no pain but only a little pleasure.

While the hedonic calculus may seem impractical, versions of the calculus are still in use. For example, NICE — the organisation which decides which treatments should be available on the NHS — considers factors such as cost and effectiveness of a drug, whether it can cure or just extend life, and how many people need it. In other words, it considers the benefits for society overall.

Political decisions can at times be made on the basis of utilitarianism. For example, abortion was legalised in 1967 on the basis that it would improve women's health. Women could get an abortion in safe medical conditions rather than have an illegal 'backstreet' abortion which might put their life at risk. These are utilitarian considerations.

Knowledge check 9

How do act utilitarians determine whether an action is moral?

Strengths and weaknesses of act utilitarianism

Strengths

Act utilitarianism may seem very self-interested, but as a theory it has a number of strengths:

- Utilitarianism is intuitive in that we naturally consider what we want to be a good thing.
- Utilitarianism can give clear answers to some moral problems (but not others).
- It is hard to ignore consequences. Actions do have effects and we should take some account of them.
- Rather than giving a blanket rule, utilitarianism puts us in a position to take circumstances into account.
- It is a secular philosophy (i.e. one unconnected with religion), which some see as a strength. Morality is created by human beings for human beings.
- It allows for the fact that different societies and cultures may have different moral codes.

Weaknesses

One of the main problems with act utilitarianism is Bentham's hedonic calculus:

- It does not consider the *quality* of the pleasures and pains. Bentham argued that pushpin (a popular pub game at the time) was as good as poetry and should be treated equally on the hedonic calculus.
- It is hard to use in practice. Can we really decide on the remoteness, intensity, purity and so on of an action and how it will affect other people?
- Is there any single experience called 'pleasure' that we can measure? When we think of the word 'pleasure', do we mean one singular sensation or several sensations?

Even if we bypass problems with the calculus, there are still problems with this approach to ethics:

■ It is not really possible to consider all the consequences of an action. We might be able to do this for a minor action that involves only one or two people, but an action that involves more people or a more serious moral situation could produce unforeseen consequences that we simply can't calculate with the information available to us.

■ Act A and act B might both result in the same amount of happiness, but act A involves telling a lie and act B does not. For an act utilitarian there is nothing to choose between these two acts, but surely we would argue that it is better not to tell a lie than to tell one?

■ Bentham's theory runs into trouble when it condones actions which are generally held to be morally inexcusable. For example, a group of prison guards are torturing a prisoner. If the guards' pleasure outweighs the prisoner's pain then, according to the hedonic calculus, their action is justified.

■ Basing moral decisions on the principle of utility could lead to injustice and the denial of individual rights. For example, a serial killer is on the loose and the town is paralysed with fear. The townsfolk are filling the streets demanding that something be done. The police have no idea who the killer is so they pick a former convict, who, although innocent of this crime, has committed crimes in the past. They put him on trial and convict him. The townsfolk are relieved and go home. It seems unjust to most people that an innocent man should be arrested, tried and convicted solely on the basis that the majority of people will be pleased by his arrest.

■ Finally, most of us agree that we have special responsibilities to particular people. However, if you saw two people drowning, one your father and the other a renowned cancer specialist, utilitarianism would suggest that you should save the doctor.

John Stuart Mill revised Bentham's theory to try to overcome some of these problems, as discussed below. You can find a Key thinker box on Mill in the section on equality (p. 20).

Mill's utilitarianism

Inspired by Bentham, Mill was a classical hedonistic utilitarian who argued that pleasure is the sole good and that the promotion of pleasure over pain should determine our moral decisions. In *Utilitarianism* (1863), Mill adapted Bentham's utilitarianism in two important ways: assessing pleasure in a qualitative way which contrasts higher and lower pleasures, and adding a framework of moral rules. These adaptations are discussed below.

Higher and lower pleasures

Mill rejected Bentham's quantitative assessment of pleasure in the hedonic calculus and replaced it with a qualitative measure. Whereas Bentham argued that one form of happiness was no more important than another, Mill put greater stress on the variety of pleasures and distinguished between their respective values. He maintained that some pleasures, those of the mind, are higher and more estimable than others, namely those of the body.

This qualitative approach solves the problem of the principle of utility justifying immoral acts: the pleasure experienced by the sadistic guards does not make the

Key quotation

It is better to be a human being dissatisfied than a pig satisfied; better to be Socrates dissatisfied than a fool satisfied. And if the fool, or the pig, is of a different opinion, it is only because they only know their own side of the question.

J. S. Mill

action moral because this particular type of pleasure is of such a low value that it does not outweigh the acute pain experienced by the prisoner.

How are we to distinguish between the two orders of pleasure? Mill says we should look to 'competent judges' who have experienced both kinds of pleasure. An opinion poll among these judges, according to Mill, would reveal that they consistently choose the pleasures of the intellect in preference to the 'lower' pleasures like eating or sex. We can enjoy lower pleasures, but the pleasures of the mind are inherently more valuable.

A moral framework

While Bentham argued against the idea of a set of rules to govern behaviour, Mill argued that a behavioural code or rule is morally right if the consequences of adopting that rule are more favourable than unfavourable to everyone. So, while Bentham's act utilitarianism weighs the consequences of each particular action, **rule utilitarianism** offers a framework of moral rules which will have favourable consequences for everyone. Adopting a rule that says 'You should not kill another person' will create more happiness for the majority as people will not be killed and will not be afraid of being killed.

Strengths and weaknesses of rule utilitarianism

Strengths

- Rule utilitarianism avoids the need to use the hedonic calculus and the need to make complex calculations in order to make a moral decision. The rule utilitarian can simply appeal to a rule, such as 'Do not steal'. Rule utilitarians only ask that, when we create the rules, we promote those rules that result in the greatest good for the greatest number. We can select, revise and replace these rules on the basis of their utility and in this way the principle of utility remains the ultimate standard.
- Rule utilitarianism respects people's liberties and rights. Mill argued that utilitarianism is compatible with classical liberal principles in that the happiest or most flourishing society would be one where people are allowed to do what they want and pursue their own interests without interference, as long as they don't harm others. Mill called this the '**harm principle**'.
- Act utilitarianism can, in certain circumstances, justify immoral actions. Rule utilitarianism avoids this in two ways. First, it focuses on general rules rather than individual actions. Act utilitarianism may justify individual acts of stealing, for example, but rule utilitarianism would have a blanket rule against stealing because prohibiting stealing has positive consequences for the whole of society. Second, rule utilitarianism argues for quality rather than quantity. The pleasure prison guards gain from torturing a prisoner can never equal the pleasure of setting up a fair-trade business.

Weaknesses

- Higher and lower pleasures are hard to define and hard to separate. Is listening to rap music less of a higher pleasure than listening to classical music? Is eating an elaborate meal less good than reading commercial romantic fiction?
- Who is a 'competent judge'? Mill argues that they are people experienced in both pleasures who can justify why some pleasures are higher. By this definition, Mill's

Rule utilitarianism A variant of utilitarianism based on a set of rules created using the principle of utility in order to give a framework for moral decision-making.

Knowledge check 10
Is rule utilitarianism a hedonistic theory, like act utilitarianism?

Harm principle J. S. Mill's liberal principle that individuals should be free to do as they wish as long as they do not harm others or their interests.

judges are educated people. Mill's theory is arguably elitist. People who are poorly educated and living in poverty may not have had the opportunity to experience what Mill characterises as 'higher' pleasures.

■ There is a possible contradiction between the consequentialist element of rule utilitarianism and its focus on following rules. Once a rule has been decided based on utility, do we abide by the rule because it is the rule or do we have in mind the fact that stealing has negative consequences? If we follow the rule because it is the rule, then arguably rule utilitarianism is not utilitarianism at all because it has become a matter of duty or intention rather than consequence. If we don't steal because of the consequences, then the rule itself becomes unnecessary.

■ What happens if I want to break the rule because breaking the rule has more utility than obeying the rule? For example, there is a clear rule against killing, but I may have to kill in self-defence. In that case I break the rule because it leads to greater happiness. If there are exceptions to a rule, is there really a rule at all?

The experience machine

Both act and rule utilitarianism face problems as hedonistic arguments based on pleasure as the criterion of moral goodness. In *Anarchy, State and Utopia* (1974), the American philosopher Robert Nozick (1939–2002) asks us to imagine an experience machine that can give us any pleasurable experience we want. For example, you could think or feel that you were writing a great novel, unaware that you're actually in a machine. Would you plug in?

Classical utilitarians would argue that we should plug into the machine as this will promote pleasure and happiness for the majority of people. However, Nozick gives us three reasons not to plug in:

■ We want actually to do things and not just have the experience of doing them.
■ We want to be a certain sort of person, not 'a blob' floating in a tank.
■ Plugging into the machine limits us to a man-made reality and limits the reality that we can make.

By considering plugging into the machine and then rejecting the idea, we demonstrate that there are other values that matter to our wellbeing as well as pleasure/happiness. Religious believers, for example, would argue that self-sacrifice, suffering and unhappiness can at times have a greater moral value as they allow you to grow spiritually and get closer to God.

Modern arguments have tended to abandon the hedonism of classical utilitarianism while retaining the consequentialist element.

Preference utilitarianism

See also the Key thinker box on Peter Singer in the section on environmental issues (p. 16).

Singer argues that hedonistic utilitarianism, with its emphasis on pleasure, does not take into account the different views people have on what constitutes pleasure and pain and the different views individuals have regarding happiness. **Preference utilitarianism** aims to solve this problem by arguing that you should take into account the preferences of the person concerned in each case, unless those preferences are outweighed by the preferences of other people. In other words, the right thing to do is

Preference utilitarianism
A modern version of utilitarianism which argues that an action should be judged on the extent to which it conforms to the preferences of those involved rather than the pleasure it produces.

the act that maximises the satisfaction of the preferences of all the people involved. For example, lying is wrong because it goes against the preference most people have to know the truth.

Preference, for Singer, also refers to 'best interests'. In other words, sometimes our pleasure or preference is tempered by what is in our best interest to do. For example, sitting an exam might not be a person's preference but it is in their long-term best interest to gain qualifications.

Strengths and weaknesses of preference utilitarianism

Strengths

- Preference utilitarianism doesn't attempt to calculate pleasure or happiness. Instead it asks people what they prefer and what they think is in their best interests.
- I know best what my preferences and interests are. Under the principle of utility, I may have to give up my preferences for the sake of the majority. This is a problem preference utilitarianism avoids.
- It allows people to speak up for themselves and defend their rights. It starts with the individual rather than with society.
- It acknowledges that not all situations are identical. People's preferences and interests may change depending on the situation.

Weaknesses

- What if a community had a preference for perversion or cruelty? As long as the preferences of those involved are being satisfied, it would seem that preference utilitarianism can justify morally questionable acts.
- Preference utilitarianism still does not solve the problem of how we decide what the consequences of the action might be and it cannot take into account all the consequences of an action.
- The preferences of the many may outweigh the preference of the one. If a woman wishes to have an abortion but all her friends and family are against it, what happens?
- What if someone is not in a position to express their preference, for example a baby or someone with dementia?
- Do I choose what I prefer now or what I would prefer in the long run if I knew all the facts? I may prefer now to smoke and take no exercise, but this is hardly in my long-term interest.
- Preference utilitarianism is incompatible with religious approaches to ethics. Religious believers may view suffering and unhappiness as meaningful because they are a test from God and so has greater moral value than human preferences. Joni Eareckson Tada has stated that soon after her accident she would have preferred to die, but with time found meaning in her hardship as it brought her closer to God.

Negative utilitarianism

Another modern form of utilitarianism is **negative utilitarianism**, first proposed by Karl Popper (1902–94). Popper agreed that morality should be based on seeking

Negative utilitarianism A form of utilitarianism that first seeks to avoid pain before seeking happiness.

pleasure and avoiding pain, but argued that there is no clear symmetry between pleasure and pain. We should aim to minimise pain and suffering first rather than seek happiness. Popper believed that the role of the state and public policy is first to minimise suffering, whereas happiness is essentially a private matter. Public resources should be directed first towards reducing the pain of hunger and poverty.

It has been argued that, taken to its logical conclusion, negative utilitarianism could lead to mass euthanasia: after all, the best way to avoid suffering and minimise pain would be to ensure the end of the world and the quick termination of all future suffering.

Ideal utilitarianism

Proposed by G. E. Moore (1873–1958), **ideal utilitarianism**, like most forms of utilitarianism, is concerned with maximising the good, but it differs in its view of what the 'good' is. Unlike hedonistic utilitarianism, it is not concerned only with pleasure or happiness, but also with other intrinsic goods, such as beauty or knowledge. A great work of art, for instance, is valuable in itself, not merely because it brings pleasure to those who appreciate it.

Ideal utilitarianism A form of utilitarianism that takes into account intrinsic benefits like beauty or knowledge, not just pleasure.

Ideal utilitarianism denies that the sole object of moral concern is hedonism — the maximising of pleasure or happiness. It considers other morally significant consequences, which are not necessarily pleasing or painful. Certain things can be unpleasant but good in themselves, such as chemotherapy. Other things that seem pleasant at first, such as smoking or getting drunk, are wrong in themselves because they cause long-term harm.

Utilitarianism: summary

- Utilitarianism is a consequentialist theory of ethics.
- Act utilitarianism is a form of hedonistic utilitarianism because it promotes pleasure/happiness as the greatest good. It weighs the effects of an action on the principle of utility: whether it brings about the greatest good for the greatest number.
- Jeremy Bentham devised the hedonic calculus as a way of calculating what action should be taken in any given situation.
- Rule utilitarianism, proposed by J. S. Mill, shares with act utilitarianism the hedonistic view that human nature is about self-interest and that we naturally seek pleasure and avoid pain. Like act utilitarianism, it is based on the principle of utility. However, rule utilitarianism rejects the hedonic calculus and the focus on individual actions in favour of general rules of behaviour, chosen on the basis of their utility.

- The rule utilitarian's assessment of pleasure is qualitative rather than quantitative. It also makes a distinction between higher and lower pleasures. The framework of rules and the distinction between higher and lower pleasures allow rule utilitarianism to overcome a key weakness of act utilitarianism: that it can be used to justify actions that most people would judge immoral.
- Modern forms of utilitarianism reject the hedonistic element. Preference utilitarianism argues that morality should be about maximising the preferences and interests of the greatest number of people. Negative utilitarianism argues that we should aim to minimise pain and suffering first rather than seek happiness. Ideal utilitarianism argues that morality should be about considering the consequences of actions with reference to what has intrinsic value, such as friendship and beauty.

Situation ethics

Situation ethics is a liberal Christian theory of ethics which argues that the central concern of ethics should be agape, or selfless love, which was the main message of Jesus's teachings.

A strength of utilitarianism, a secular theory of ethics, is its flexibility. Its weakness is that it fails to give clear guidelines for behaviour and can even, at times, justify immoral actions.

Natural law theory or natural moral law, a religious perspective on ethics, gives clear guidelines for behaviour but is arguably too absolutist — it doesn't take into account exceptions and is unworkable in modern secular societies which allow sex before marriage, abortion and gay marriage. As an essentially Christian theory of ethics that aims to be more flexible and more in tune with contemporary society, situation ethics to some extent bridges these two approaches.

Social, political and cultural influences

Situation ethics had its origins in the USA of the 1960s when both society and the Christian Church were facing radical change. The USA was engaged in the Vietnam War, President Kennedy had been assassinated in 1963 and Martin Luther King was leading the civil rights movement. Meanwhile, women had gained greater independence after the Second World War and this trend accelerated as more and more men went to fight in Vietnam.

What really led to a shift in Christian moral thinking, however, was the sexual revolution that took place against this political background. For example, the use of contraceptives became legal for married couples in 1965 and for unmarried couples in 1972; in 1973 abortion was legalised in the USA. Under Donald Trump's presidency there have been signs of a hardening of attitudes towards abortion in some states.

The liberal principles behind these changes, and the greater focus on gender and racial equality, were welcomed overall. However, the Church was concerned that it would lead to moral degradation. In the UK, in 1966, the British Council of Churches published the report *Sex and Morality*, in which it shared its concerns about changing attitudes to sex, marriage and family. The Council presented a case for abstinence from pre-marital sexual intercourse and suggested that courses in human relationships be included in the school curriculum. It felt that young people needed more guidance concerning sexual relationships at a time when they were gaining more freedom, family bonds were weakening and religion was playing a lesser role in everyday life.

It was within this context that J. A. T. Robinson, an English theologian, and Joseph Fletcher, an American professor, decided to reassess Christian ethics and propose a 'new morality'.

J. A. T. Robinson's situationism

In *Honest to God*, Robinson argued that we should stop thinking about God as a remote, transcendent being but instead see God as part of our lives and the ground of our being. Robinson's aim was to demythologise God and make religious arguments fit with modern science within the spirit of the Bible. He argued that religion had to

Natural law theory
A form of divine command theory, this is the argument that everything in the universe shows purpose. God creates rational moral laws for us to follow; we work them out using reason.

Key quotation

The ruling norm of Christian decision is love: nothing else.

Joseph Fletcher

change in order to respond effectively to the atheist argument that religious truths are simply myths. This meant changing the Christian view on ethics. Robinson scandalised some people with his argument that sex was an act of holy communion and with his acceptance of divorce. He felt that humankind had come of age and that people were rational beings and should be free to make their own moral decisions.

Key thinker

J. A. T. Robinson (1919–83)

The Anglican bishop of Woolwich, English New Testament scholar and author, Robinson argued for a liberalisation of Christian ethics in his most famous work, *Honest to God*, published in 1963.

Robinson felt that the true message of the New Testament is one of compassion, acceptance and, particularly, love. Robinson was a New Testament scholar and believed that Jesus was himself a supporter of a new morality. For example, in Mark 12, a scribe asks Jesus which is the most important commandment:

> Jesus answered, the first is this, Hear, O Israel; The Lord our God, the Lord is one; and you shall love the Lord thy God with all your heart and with all your soul, and with all your mind, and with all your strength. The second is this, you shall love your neighbour as yourself. There is no other commandment greater than these.

Mark 12:29–31

In Matthew 23, Jesus condemns the Pharisees, a Jewish sect very strict in its observance of religious laws. He argues against basing moral principles on the Torah and instead argues for a more situationist approach. Absolute rules cannot apply to every situation; we should consider each situation individually and use love, charity and compassion to make moral decisions.

Agape

Situationists call this love by the Greek word *agape*: the greatest love, a love that is selfless and unconditional. This type of love is distinct from romantic love (*eros*) and the love we feel towards our family and friends (*philia*). It is an attitude towards others rather than a feeling. We could show agape love towards our enemies if we forgive them, for example. Agape love doesn't change, whether it is returned or not, and implies total commitment.

For Robinson, agape is the only moral law we should follow. **Divine command theory** doesn't make sense. We should consider situations case by case, and determine what the most loving decision is, rather than obey a universal and absolute moral code.

How does this work in practice, though? At the time, divorce was considered immoral because marriage was regarded as a spiritual bond between two people and breaking that bond went against God's absolute command. The conservative view on divorce is clear: the union is metaphysical and only God can dissolve it.

Key quotations

Owe no one anything, except to love one another, for the one who loves another has fulfilled the law.

Romans 13:8

Love does no wrong to a neighbour; therefore love is the fulfilling of the law.

Romans 13:10

Divine command theory An ethical theory which states that whatever God commands is good: moral codes are universal and absolute.

Robinson sought to show that there is nothing fundamentally immoral or unchristian about divorce. Indeed, divorce can sometimes be the moral choice. A marriage may be violent, or one or both partners may have stopped loving and respecting the other. Breaking the bond can be selfless rather than selfish: a person may be thinking of the long-term happiness of their partner and children, for example.

But how do we know that the decision we have taken is the most loving? I may find divorcing my partner to be the most loving thing for them and my children, but they may disagree and think the most loving thing is to remain married. And aren't some things simply wrong under any circumstance, for example child abuse?

Joseph Fletcher attempted to make the application of situation ethics clearer and more practical.

Fletcher's situationism

Fletcher agrees with Robinson that Jesus's approach to ethics is fundamentally situationist, but Fletcher's argument and defence of situationism are arguably more philosophically sound and systematic. Fletcher first explains where situation ethics stands in relation to other ethical theories, then proposes a system of principles to help us make moral decisions and solve moral dilemmas.

> **Key thinker**
>
> **Joseph Fletcher (1905–91)**
> Fletcher was an American episcopal priest and professor of biomedical ethics who argued for a situationist and consequentialist perspective on religious morality. He wrote his famous book *Situation Ethics* in 1966, three years after Robinson's *Honest to God*. In the late 1960s, however, he became an atheist and began to espouse humanism in ethics.

Situationism, legalism and antinomianism

Fletcher argues that situation ethics is the third approach and lies in between legalism and antinomianism in ethics.

Legalism in ethics refers to prefabricated moral rules, codes and regulations. Divine command theory is an example of legalism, as is natural law theory. According to Fletcher, the main problem with legalism is that it is too inflexible and that rules are too general to be able to take into account specific ethical situations. For example, the commandment not to kill is absolute, but what if we need to kill in war, in self-defence? What about abortion or withdrawal of life support if the person has no prospect of recovery? We could create more laws to take account of particular problems, but this may lead to conflicting rules and laws. For Fletcher, both Catholic and Protestant churches are guilty of obeying religious principles at the expense of what truly matters, which is agape love.

Antinomianism is a completely relativistic theory of ethics — according to antinomianism, there should be no rule whatsoever. Every situation is unique and we should do what feels right at the time. There is no duty or requirement to be consistent and there are no principles to follow.

Knowledge check 11

What does 'agape' mean?

Key quotation

Love relativizes the absolute, it does not absolutize the relative.

Joseph Fletcher

Key quotation

Only one thing is intrinsically good, namely love, nothing else at all.

Joseph Fletcher

Situation ethics stands in the middle: it rejects the absolutism of legalism but also the unprincipled relativism of antinomianism. It is more concerned with love than with rules. Fletcher is not arguing that we should forfeit commandments and religious codes, but argues that we should not obey rules for their own sake. We should put such codes and practices aside if they conflict with the law of love and prevent agape. This approach doesn't relinquish legalism completely — love itself is a law and, most of the time, we should obey religious commands — but it also values individual freedom and accounts for the fact that every situation is different.

Love and justice

Fletcher argues that love and justice are the same. Love is self-giving and overrides all laws so it may, for example, give permission to kill if that is the most loving action. Justice follows from love and love put into practice can only result in justice. Love means willing my neighbour's good even if I don't like him or her. There can be no love without justice. Injustices such as a child starving or a man arrested without charge are examples of a lack of love. If love was properly shared out, there would be no injustice.

That leads Fletcher to argue that justice is love distributed. That implies there are no absolute laws other than the law of agape love; all the other laws are secondary, as the only way to achieve true justice is by choosing the most loving action. When love and justice are opposed, one has to choose one or the other. Where justice is love distributed, everyone's interests are taken into account.

Principles of situation ethics

Situation ethics fundamentally relies on one principle: agape. All moral decisions depend on what is the most loving thing to do. However, this needs to be workable in practice, so Fletcher created ten principles to make situation ethics as practical as possible. He split these into four working presuppositions and six fundamental principles.

Four working presuppositions

Fletcher's four working presuppositions are as follows:

- Pragmatism — an action must work in practice.
- Relativism — there are no fixed rules; the only principle is agape.
- Positivism — making a decision is about wanting to do the right thing, not obeying a command or using reason.
- Personalism — human beings are more important than rules.

Six fundamental principles

The six principles or presuppositions that Fletcher sees as fundamental to ethics are as follows:

- Agape love is the absolute norm, the main point of reference in moral decision-making.
- Love overrides all other laws.
- Justice is part of love, so it is moral to break laws if they serve love.
- Love has no favourite; it is selfless and doesn't give preferential treatment.
- Love is the end, not a means to an end, for example money or power.
- The loving thing to do is relative to the situation.

> **Key quotation**
>
> Love and justice are the same, for love is justice distributed, nothing else.
>
> Joseph Fletcher

> **Knowledge check 12**
>
> In what way are utilitarianism and situation ethics similar?

Case studies

In the appendix to *Situation Ethics*, Fletcher gives four case studies. Although we do not know the outcomes (apart from the bombing of Hiroshima and Nagasaki), Fletcher wants to show that this way of thinking about morality can offer solutions.

- The defence agency asks a young woman to work undercover and 'involve' a married man working for a rival power. They argue that her self-sacrifice is no different to her brother risking his life fighting in Korea. How can she balance patriotic duty with her own ideal of sexual integrity?
- A married German woman with three children is told that she can only be released from a Soviet POW camp if she is pregnant. She asks a camp guard to make her pregnant. Her family welcome her and the baby home, but is it moral to christen the baby?
- A terminally ill man with six months to live could opt for treatment that might keep him alive for three years. However, his life insurance policy expires the following October. If he accepts the treatment and lives past October, his family will be left in dire straits when he eventually dies. Should he accept the treatment?
- Could the ending of the Second World War justify the killing and injuring of hundreds of thousands of innocent people by dropping nuclear bombs on Hiroshima and Nagasaki?

Strengths of situation ethics

- Situation ethics is a strong theory: it combines the positives of **deontological** thinking in that there is an overarching principle to follow — agape love — with consequentialist thinking. It is simple, effective, pragmatic and practical. It avoids justifying what we would consider immoral actions, something utilitarianism struggles with, and it is flexible. Killing, for example, may be morally permissible in one case but not in another.
- It gives us moral responsibility. With divine command ethics, we have to follow and obey God; here, we are moral agents in charge of our moral decisions.
- It is consistent with the overall message of the New Testament but at the same time is compatible with a secular, more liberal way of thinking about ethics. It provides a way for people to make decisions about issues not addressed in the Bible, such as birth control and genetic engineering.

Weaknesses of situation ethics: William Barclay

> ### Key thinker
>
> #### William Barclay (1907–78)
> Barclay was a Church of Scotland minister and scholar and taught at the University of Glasgow for 28 years. He was widely known in Britain for his radio and television broadcasts. His many books included *Ethics in a Permissive Society* (1971), which included a critique of situation ethics.

Barclay's first criticism is that Fletcher's examples are far-fetched. Situation ethics may be the best approach in extraordinary situations but that doesn't justify choosing it for everyday morality.

> **Knowledge check 13**
>
> Give an example of an action that would run counter to divine command theory but be acceptable to a situationist.

> **Deontological** Relating to duty.

> **Exam tip**
>
> Barclay's 'Situation Ethics' is a prescribed anthology text. Use this link to access the *Anthology*: https://tinyurl.com/yargzcu6
>
> Section B of Paper 2 will consist of a two-part question on an excerpt from an anthology text.

Barclay also thinks that situation ethics gives human beings too much freedom in their moral decision-making, a freedom we do not actually want. People don't automatically know what to do, and 'prefabricated judgements' — moral guidelines — are vital to our decision-making. Fletcher would object to this criticism, however. He argues that we should follow moral principles but that sometimes we need to break them, as in his four case studies. The rule of agape is a form of guidance, even though it is flexible, and his principles and presuppositions are there to help us make moral decisions.

Barclay's main issue with situation ethics is the fact that, with no clear moral absolutes to base our decisions on, it could justify any action, even those that we would consider clearly immoral.

Barclay adds that mankind is not yet rational enough ('has not come of age') to make independent decisions. We need clear moral guidelines to distinguish between right and wrong. We need 'the protection of law', and that may simply mean being forced to obey the law.

Barclay is also critical of situation ethics for the idea that the good is determined by the action, rather than us judging the action by existing moral standards. For Barclay, certain things are inherently wrong: he gives the example of drug addiction brought about because a young person wanted to experiment, and that of adultery, carried out in the name of love yet breaking up a family. We can and should sublimate our desires into something moral. Situation ethics, says Barclay, forgets that human beings can overcome certain desires and avoid breaking the moral law, because of the grace of God (God's ability to show mercy and forgive).

Public and private morality

Finally, Barclay draws on the longstanding distinction in philosophy between private and public morality. The law focuses on public morality — what people do in public that could affect society, for example driving while drunk. Private morality refers to what we do in private which arguably doesn't affect the wider society, for example getting drunk in the privacy of your own home.

Liberal thinkers argue that the state should have no say in what we do in private. Barclay refers to the 1957 Wolfenden Report, which sought to decriminalise homosexuality in England and Wales. H. L. A. Hart, a law professor, argued that because homosexuality is a self-regarding action, it is not detrimental to society and should be made legal. Lord Devlin, a judge with more conservative views, argued that, on the contrary, there is no such thing as private morality and self-regarding actions; our private choices, especially when they are moral choices, will have an effect on our immediate acquaintances. In his opinion, activities that threaten society's norms and public morality threaten society as a whole and should therefore be punished. Homosexuality was not decriminalised until 1967.

As a conservative Christian thinker, Barclay is opposed to the idea that there is a private sphere. What we do in private has an effect in society — no man is an island.

While Fletcher argues that moral responsibility can only come about if we are completely free, Barclay argues that no one is completely free: we are determined by society, our immediate environment, our heredity and any decisions we made previously. There is therefore a tension between freedom and law. He also makes a separate point about moral responsibility: responsibility is as much about deciding what *not* to do as it is about deciding what to do. We are free to act but also not to act.

Key quotation

Freedom can become licence.

William Barclay

Key quotation

The situationist is less than realistic in the extent to which he is willing to recognise the weakness of human nature and the fact that even our conscience can be distorted.

William Barclay

Is situation ethics compatible with religion?

Even though it is rooted in Christian principles, situation ethics has been rejected by the Roman Catholic Church and the majority of the Anglican community because it does not accurately reflect New Testament views on morality, especially on theft and adultery. Roman Catholic leaders have argued that situation ethics is too individualistic to reflect the teachings of the Bible: it is wrong to appeal to individual circumstances in an attempt to justify what clearly goes, at times, against the teachings of the Church.

Situation ethics: summary

- Drawing on the New Testament, the Christian scholar J. A. T. Robinson argued for a liberalisation of ethics based on the principle of agape, or selfless, unconditional love.
- Situation ethics rejects both legalism, which implies a set of absolute inflexible rules, and antinomianism, which means complete freedom of choice, in favour of a flexible system of thought with one aim: to promote the rule of agape, or unconditional love. In situation ethics, right and wrong depend on the situation. There are no universal moral rules or rights.
- Joseph Fletcher formulated principles and presuppositions to demonstrate that morality can be both universal and practical.

- The theory has been criticised on the basis that it betrays Christian ethical principles and can at times justify immoral actions.
- William Barclay is very critical of situation ethics as giving human beings too much freedom so that we end up not knowing what to do. This freedom may also justify immoral actions. Even if carried out with good intentions, actions like adultery go against Christian moral principles and can threaten the stability of society.
- Situation ethics could now be considered outdated: it is deeply rooted in 1960s' new liberal thinking, when its main function was to show that it was possible to be a committed Christian in a secular liberal world.

Natural moral law

Natural moral law is a form of divine command theory. It is a theory of ethics traditionally associated with Christianity — and is followed by the Roman Catholic Church — but it is universal in its scope. It argues that God created the universe according to rational principles and that nature is ordered. Humans, created in the image of God, have reason and can use their rationality to discover the laws and rules of nature. The universe, as created by God, is moral; humans just need to look at the natural world and, using reason, can work out how to be moral beings.

The Christian ethical view

The Christian approach to ethics sees motives and duty as the source of morality, not consequences, as in utilitarianism. In Christian ethics, we have a duty to ourselves, but also a duty to God in so far as we need to be the best person we can be. Being a good person brings eschatological rewards — rewards in the afterlife.

According to the Christian moral view, there cannot be a moral standard of good independent of God. Christian ethics, and particularly natural moral law, is absolutist and legalist:

- It advocates *absolute* moral rules, which allow no exceptions: this is because they are God-given and to allow for exceptions would imply that the commands are not perfect.
- It is *legalist* in that it gives us a clear moral code to follow, similar to rules of law.

However, we should not follow God's will because of fear of punishment or because we want to earn his favour — that would make him no more than a tyrant.

The origins of natural law

Aristotle is often considered to be the founder of natural law.

> **Key thinker**
>
> ### Aristotle (384–322 BCE)
> Aristotle was born in Stagira, on the northern coast of Greece, and was the son of the doctor to Philip of Macedonia. A student of Plato, Aristotle studied at the Academy in Athens for 20 years. Plato called Aristotle the 'Mind' because he was always reading. Aristotle became tutor to the young Alexander before returning to Athens in 335 BCE to set up the Lyceum, his school and research institute. Aristotle studied and wrote on almost every field of human knowledge, from biology to poetry and politics, and has profoundly influenced Western thought (and some Eastern thought too).

Key quotation

Every craft and every investigation, and likewise every action and decision, seems to aim at some good; hence the good has been well described as that at which everything aims.

Aristotle

Aristotle argued that although humans follow the customs and laws of society, there is also a universal law which we can all abide by — the law of nature. Human beings have a specific function that no other animal has, and that is reason. Reason goes beyond the rules of society and is universal. To flourish, we must fulfil our function and use our reason well.

Natural law is based on Aristotle's idea that everything has a purpose (*telos*), revealed in its design (or natural 'form'), and that the fulfilment of the *telos* is the supreme 'good' to be sought.

Telos Greek word meaning 'end' or 'purpose'.

Aquinas adapted Aristotle's theory to make it fit with a Christian world-view.

Aquinas's natural law theory

> **Key thinker**
>
> ### St Thomas Aquinas (1224–74)
> Thomas Aquinas was a priest of the Roman Catholic Church and a Dominican friar. A foremost proponent of natural theology, he is considered by many Catholics to be the Church's greatest theologian and philosopher. His influence on Western thought has been considerable, and much of modern philosophy has been conceived as a reaction against, or as an agreement with, his ideas, particularly in the areas of ethics, natural law and political theory. In his writings he argued that reason and faith do not conflict because both are God-given.

Aquinas combines biblical and classical influences:

■ revelation — how God reveals himself in the Bible
■ natural theology — the study of God from a philosophical, rational point of view

Aquinas argues that the world is ordered and rational; everything in the universe has a *telos*, a purpose. God is a necessary being who has created a contingent world, which shows order and purpose but also characteristics of a divine will. God didn't create the universe by chance, as that would be contrary to his nature; the created world happened for a reason. For Aquinas, the creation of the world reveals God's goodness and that implies that what is in the universe is also good and has a purpose. The universe follows certain rational rules, which Aquinas calls natural laws.

Unlike non-human beings, humans have free will, which means they have choice and responsibility. They also have reason. Like Aristotle, Aquinas argues that the primary function of human beings is to use reason well. They must use their reason to know God and that is the ultimate fulfilment or happiness. The purpose of human beings is to find truth and in the process lead a virtuous life.

Aquinas, like Aristotle, makes a distinction between efficient and final cause:

■ An efficient cause is the agent of change which brings about its effect — in other words, what we would normally term 'the cause'.
■ The final cause is the goal or purpose towards which a thing is oriented. For Aristotle, everything has a final 'good', which is achieved by fulfilling the purpose for which it was designed — its final cause.

Natural law depends upon this distinction. It assumes (by whatever means employed) that the world is the creation of God and thus should reveal his ultimate purpose in creating it.

The purpose of natural law theory is to work out how human beings can be moral. An action is good if it contributes to our purpose or *telos*. For Aquinas our *telos* is to gain an understanding of God, to be closer to God.

Primary and secondary precepts

Aquinas starts with a single guiding principle that sums up our nature: we must do good and avoid evil. All **precepts** of the natural law are based upon this. Aquinas identified two types of precepts: primary and secondary.

Aquinas's natural law is both **teleological** and **deontological**. The primary precepts are teleological in that they relate to human purpose; the secondary precepts are deontological in that they provide specific laws to follow.

We can work out the primary precepts of natural law by using reason and observing the natural world. Primary precepts are goods which we all seek and which contribute to human fulfilment.

There are five primary precepts:

■ preservation of life
■ reproduction/procreation
■ education
■ an ordered society
■ worship of God

Key quotation

Man has a natural inclination to know the truth about God, and to live in society: and in this respect, whatever pertains to this inclination belongs to the natural law.

Aquinas

Precept A general rule which tells us how to behave.

Teleological Relating to purpose.

Deontological Relating to duty.

The primary precepts give rise to secondary precepts which give clearer, more specific, absolute rules or laws. The primary precept of 'preservation of life', for example, gives rise to secondary precepts such as 'Do not kill'. A follower of natural law theory might also argue that assisted suicide is immoral on the grounds that it goes against the same primary precept.

Natural law theory argues against homosexuality because it goes against the primary precept of procreation.

Exterior and interior acts

Aquinas also makes a distinction between interior and exterior acts:

- An interior act is the intention behind the action.
- An exterior act is the actual act that is performed.

For an action to be good, the intention behind it as well as the act itself must be good. An action cannot be good if it is done for the wrong reasons. Giving my seat to an elderly man on the bus to impress my new girlfriend is not moral as it is done with a wrong intention. Similarly, a good intention doesn't necessarily lead to a good action: I may have the good intention to help a friend in need which leads me to steal money from my parents. Here the interior act is good but the exterior act is not.

Real and apparent goods

The function of humans is to use reason, but we don't always use our reason well. At times we follow apparent goods rather than real goods. Apparent goods go against primary and secondary precepts. For example, committing adultery is an apparent good: it may seem like a good idea, and the people involved feel some happiness, but it is not a real good as it goes against the primary precept of an ordered society.

We can distinguish between apparent and real good if we apply reason correctly. Following real goods will mean we flourish and become virtuous beings. Following apparent goods might give us pleasure but we are not fulfilling our potential as rational human beings.

The cardinal virtues

Being virtuous allows us to fulfil our purpose. Using reason, human beings can identify four main virtues which Aquinas calls cardinal virtues:

- prudence — judging correctly whether a given course of action is right or wrong
- temperance — restraining our desires or passions (not overindulging in food, for example) but not denying ourselves either
- fortitude — having courage and, while not seeking danger unnecessarily, standing up to one's fears
- justice — connected with the idea of rights, giving everyone their due

The Bible reveals three more virtues — the theological virtues of faith, hope and charity.

Aquinas also identifies seven vices (often known as the 'seven deadly sins'), which lead people away from the natural law they should know by reason: pride, avarice, lust, envy, gluttony, anger and sloth.

To keep to natural law, an individual should seek to develop the virtues and eliminate the vices, and this requires practice. The virtues must become habitual.

Knowledge check 14

Why are secondary precepts deontological in nature?

Key quotation

God Himself is the rule and mode of virtue. Our faith is measured by divine truth, our hope by the greatness of His power and faithful affection, our charity by His goodness. His truth, power and goodness outreach any measure of reason.

Aquinas

The doctrine of double effect and casuistry

What if two precepts conflict? For example, doctors have a duty of care towards their patients and a duty to preserve life, but what if their patient is terminally ill and suffering greatly?

The doctrine of double effect refers to situations where there is an intended outcome, the one that is sought, accompanied by another significant unintended outcome, which is not necessarily desirable. According to natural law, it is our intentions that are important, not the consequences of our actions. A doctor giving pain relief to a terminally ill patient has a good intention, to help the patient and relieve appalling pain. This could, in certain circumstances, hasten death, but natural law would not prevent the doctor from doing his or her utmost to relieve suffering.

Similarly, natural law is clear that abortion is immoral because it goes against the primary precept of preserving life. However, what happens if the mother's life is at risk? The doctrine of double effect can help us make a decision.

Consider a woman who has an ectopic pregnancy — that is, the embryo is growing in one of her fallopian tubes rather than in the uterus. The tube is at risk of bursting, which would put her life at risk. However, removing the embryo or the fallopian tube is, in effect, an abortion. The doctrine of double effect would argue that it is moral to remove the fallopian tube, based on the primary precept of preserving life, despite the unintended consequence that the embryo dies.

While it seems strange to pretend that consequences that we are very aware of are unintended, in such cases this is the only way to put natural law into practice.

The doctrine of double effect is closely linked to the practice of **casuistry**. Some principles have logical consequences. For example, if it is in principle wrong to kill innocent human beings, it follows that bombing civilian targets is wrong. However, if it is accepted that killing in self-defence is acceptable, it might be possible to justify an air attack on these grounds. Innocent people might die, but that is not the aim of the action, so the doctrine of double effect comes into play. (This featured prominently in President Truman's argument for choosing Hiroshima as the target for the first atomic bomb.) Another example would be that of lying: while lying is wrong according to natural law, for example lying under oath, lying would become acceptable if it was to save a life.

Casuistry Applying principles to individual cases.

Knowledge check 15

What would natural moral law have to say regarding abortion, contraception and divorce?

Strengths and weaknesses of natural law theory

Strengths

■ Natural law is a universal theory of ethics: it can be applied to any circumstance and it gives us clear guidelines that are universally applicable. It can unite cultures and religious traditions because we can all work out moral precepts through the use of reason. The values that Aquinas focuses on, such as education and preserving the species, are (with a few exceptions) universal. Aquinas wants to unite faith and reason and he sees religious teachings as fundamentally rational because they are derived from an understanding of God's true nature. However, natural law theory doesn't presuppose a belief in God: we work out what is moral using reason and through looking at the world, so in that sense it is objective.

- Aquinas' natural law takes into account that human beings have a purpose and a function in the universe. Although natural law is deontological in that it focuses on intentions and motives (as we saw with the real and apparent good), there is also a teleological element in that it looks at the goal of human life. That goal is not hedonistic, as with utilitarianism, but looks more at the fact that we want to flourish, find value in our lives and get closer to truth.

- Natural law focuses on the moral character of the agent rather than just on the action itself, as utilitarians do. Through using reason and following the precepts, a person can become virtuous. The theory gives autonomy to the individual: it allows them, using reason, to work out for themselves what is objectively right and true rather than relying on religious authority, scripture or tradition.

- Natural law allows societies to be more harmonious and cohesive through helping individual humans to achieve health, happiness, friendship and so on. It is also more flexible than it appears: it allows for secondary precepts to vary according to culture, as they are the practical working out of the universal primary precepts.

Weaknesses

- Natural law may be too simplistic in overlooking other possible traits and motivations, for example emotions and feelings, involved in making moral decisions.

- Although natural law is based on reason and in theory doesn't require a belief in God, it relies on a God-given purpose so only really makes sense to someone who believes in God as an intelligent designer who has put purpose and order in the world.

- Like utilitarianism, the theory can lead to outcomes which some might see as immoral. For example, the spread of HIV in Africa was in part due to the lack of availability of barrier contraception.

- The doctrine of double effect is more consequentialist than deontological: it looks as though we can justify terrible things if the consequences are positive.

- Natural law can lead to a conflict of duties: I have a duty not to lie, but what if the only way to save my friend is to lie?

- Arguably natural law enforces traditional views that are out of touch with twenty-first-century society. This leads to homophobia, transphobia and intolerance of other cultures and ways of life.

The philosopher Bernard Hoose has updated the theory to take into account those criticisms.

Hoose and proportionalism

Hoose feels that natural moral law needs to be simplified and made more applicable to our everyday life. Rather than lists of absolute rules we must abide by, we need a system of guidelines which we navigate for ourselves — a moral compass rather than a moral law.

Hoose accepts that certain acts are wrong or evil, but argues that in some circumstances such an act might be the right thing to do, if there is a proportionate reason. Hoose's argument is quite similar to situation ethics in that it takes a flexible approach to religious ethics. Proportionalism disregards absolutism and puts more of an emphasis on the consequences. Arguably, then, it fails to keep to the spirit of natural law theory.

Key quotation

It is never right to go against a principle unless there is a proportionate reason which would justify it.

Bernard Hoose

Hoose argues that the doctrine of double effect is useful to an extent, but it does not address the problems regarding the primary precepts. One of the precepts is to preserve life. Aquinas sees this as the most important because, if you fulfil this, you can fulfil the other precepts which follow. But what should happen to a terminally ill person who is suffering and only being kept alive through the prescription of strong medication? Natural law would not allow that the person be allowed to die, but proportionalism takes into account other virtues, such as dignity, and would allow the person to die rather than continuing to live in pain to fulfil an absolutist theory.

Key thinker

Bernard Hoose (b.1945)

Bernard Hoose is a British philosopher, theologian and lecturer in Christian ethics who argues that natural law still applies in the modern world but should be understood as a list of guidelines rather than moral absolutes.

Knowledge check 16

In what way does proportionalism resemble rule or preference utilitarianism?

Similarly, natural law would oppose techniques like *in vitro* fertilisation (IVF), as this is not a natural method of reproduction. Hoose would argue that natural law is also about a person flourishing and fulfilling the purpose they have given themselves, so we ought to allow flexibility in such a circumstance.

Natural moral law: summary

- Natural law theory is particularly associated with Aristotle and Aquinas. Aquinas argues that human nature is defined by reason and freedom: it is our ability to reason and to make our own free choices that sets us apart from other animals. Through reason we can discover what our purpose is and how to live morally and so achieve closeness to God.
- Aquinas argues that the universe obeys rational laws and that certain moral frameworks exist and form the basis of our moral codes: these are the primary precepts. Secondary precepts are absolute rules derived from the primary precepts and we must follow these in order to be moral. Good actions are based on the primary and secondary precepts, and are done with the correct intention (the interior act) in order to achieve a real rather than apparent good.
- Natural law can appear inflexible and fundamentally religious, which calls into question its universality and the possibility of its application in a more secular age.
- Bernard Hoose's proportionalism argues that natural law is a guideline for behaviour rather than a set of absolute rules.

■ Application of ethical theories to issues of importance

War and peace

'War' refers to armed conflict that takes place over a period of time and involves violence, destruction and economic instability. It can be:

- a conflict between two or more states in which war is declared by the sovereign authority
- a civil war between citizens of the same country
- guerrilla warfare, in which armed civilians or paramilitary personnel use tactics such as sabotage or ambush to fight a bigger military force

Every war is a unique situation. What we do know is that it can potentially affect millions of people, both military and civilian.

The Christian view of war

In the Old Testament, God seems to sanction the waging of war. The people of Israel were allowed to engage in warfare — but only when directed by God. The act of war was moral if it arose from a divine command:

> When you draw near to a city to fight against it, offer terms of peace to it. And if it responds to you peaceably and it opens to you, then all the people who are found in it shall do forced labour for you and shall serve you. But if it makes no peace with you, but makes war against you, then you shall besiege it. And when the Lord your God gives it into your hand, you shall put all its males to the sword, but the women and the little ones, the livestock, and everything else in the city, all its spoil, you shall take as plunder for yourselves. And you shall enjoy the spoil of your enemies, which the Lord your God has given you. Thus you shall do to all the cities that are very far from you, which are not cities of the nations here.

Deuteronomy 20:10–15

In the New Testament, war seems to be more about defeating evil:

> And when the thousand years are ended, Satan will be released from his prison and will come out to deceive the nations that are at the four corners of the earth, Gog and Magog, to gather them for battle; their number is like the sand of the sea. And they marched up over the broad plain of the earth and surrounded the camp of the saints and the beloved city, but fire came down from heaven and consumed them, and the devil who had deceived them was thrown into the lake of fire and sulfur where the beast and the false prophet were, and they will be tormented day and night forever and ever.

Revelation 20:7–10

This passage looks at the battle between good and evil from an **eschatological** perspective (see p. 13 for definition): it is about the end of the world, judgement day and the victory of God over evil.

Two main views on war dominate the history of Christianity:

- the notion of just war: the argument that, in certain situations, war can be just or moral
- pacifism: in its absolute form, the argument that war is never justified, regardless of the circumstances

The just war theory

Just war theory is an attempt to provide a moral framework for war. One of the main thinkers behind just war theory was Augustine of Hippo and some of his ideas were later developed by Aquinas.

> **Key thinker**
>
> ### St Augustine of Hippo (354–430 CE)
> St Augustine of Hippo was born in the Roman province of Thagaste in what is now Algeria. He was the bishop of Hippo Regius in north Africa and one of the most influential of the early Christian thinkers and theologians. His most important works are *The City of God*, *On Christian Doctrine* and *Confessions*. His thoughts and views profoundly influenced the medieval view of the world and man's place in it.

See also the Key thinker box on St Thomas Aquinas in the section on natural moral law (p. 41).

Augustine lived at a time when parts of the Roman Empire were under threat, which made him consider the morality of war and whether there could be moral values embedded in the pursuit and undertaking of war. Augustine considered:

- *jus ad bellum* — just cause for war
- *jus in bello* — just conduct in war

Modern theorists have added a third perspective:

- *jus post bellum* — the right conduct after the war

Jus ad bellum

Augustine identified four criteria in order to decide whether a nation has a moral right to go to war against another:

- Just cause — a war can only be waged for a good reason, for example to protect a country's citizens and its land or to prevent attack.
- Last resort — war should be considered only after all other avenues have been explored.
- Legitimate authority — the decision to go to war must be made by a legitimate authority, such as an elected government.
- Right intention — why do we want to go to war? To conquer or to achieve peace? For Augustine the only right intention is to seek the good and to overcome evil.

Key quotation

True religion looks upon as peaceful those wars that are waged not for motives of aggrandisement or cruelty, but with the object of securing peace, of punishing evil-doers, and of uplifting the good.

Augustine

Key quotation

We do not seek peace in order to be at war, but go to war that we may have peace.

Augustine

Aquinas later added a fifth criterion:

■ Probability of success — for a war to be just, the chances of it achieving its aims must be significant.

Just cause

This is perhaps the most important criterion. A just war may be waged in response to an act of aggression already committed or to pre-empt one that is anticipated. Utilitarians would argue that a pre-emptive strike deters aggressors and therefore secures the greatest happiness for the greatest number, but a pre-emptive strike is, by its very nature, based on conjecture. Posturing and the build-up of arms do not necessarily constitute aggression: a man carrying a weapon is not the same as a man using a weapon.

Last resort

In just war theory it is important to attempt to resolve the situation through all means possible before war. This could include diplomacy. One of the problems with the allied invasion of Iraq in 2003 was that not every alternative means had been explored before the US-led forces invaded.

Legitimate authority

Last resort links to the criterion of proper authority. In the case of Iraq, the USA and the UK argued that their alliance had legitimate authority to invade based on UN resolutions and that, as the governments of each country had been democratically elected, they could legitimately argue that they had the authority to take their countries to war. However, this claim of legitimate authority has been highly controversial.

Right intention

The possession of right intention is, on the face of it, less problematic. If a nation wages war for a just cause then the war will be fought with the right intention, but if a war is fought out of self-interest this undermines any sense of justice. The accusation that the UK and the USA invaded Iraq purely to safeguard Iraqi oil would, were it true, identify a wrong intention and would eliminate any just cause for the war.

Probability of success

If there is a just cause and the right intention, the just war theorist also argues that there should be a chance of reasonable success, yet many wars begin without the hope of success. In 1940 Stalin's Russia invaded Finland. The likelihood of the Finns succeeding in defeating their enormous neighbour seemed remote, but does this mean that the Finns should not have undertaken the war? Sometimes, it would seem, it is morally necessary to stand up to an aggressive neighbour or to fight even when it seems that victory is not possible.

Jus in bello

Is it really possible to have just conduct in war? Here three criteria apply: discrimination, proportionality and responsibility.

Discrimination

Discrimination concerns the question of who is a legitimate target in war. It is unjust to attack indiscriminately, as non-combatants are outside the field of war. But who is

Exam tip

Examiners like to see a deep engagement with ideas in students' writing. Making connections between the themes of the course and current affairs will help you to write more analytic and evaluative essays.

a non-combatant? Is there a point when a non-combatant becomes a combatant? This issue becomes even more difficult when wars are waged in urban environments, such as Beirut or Damascus.

Proportionality

Any offensive action should be proportional to the objective desired, with minimal destruction and casualties. This position is broadly utilitarian in that it seeks to minimise overall suffering. The implication is that only military targets should be attacked as this would minimise overall suffering and restrict damage to legitimate targets.

The question of proportionality might lead us to consider other ways of concluding hostilities. However, most just war theorists would argue that covert operations are not justified as (consequentialists would argue) the enemy is likely to retaliate in the same way and ultimately more harm could result.

Responsibility

Should a nation be accountable for unforeseen damages or consequences if the intention was to produce good consequences and the bad effects were not intended? Does the good of the war outweigh the damage inflicted?

We also need to consider the morality of obeying orders when one knows those orders to be immoral. During the Nuremberg trials of leading Nazis in 1945 and 1946, and in Adolf Eichmann's trial in 1961, part of the charge was that these men knew that what they were doing was immoral and wrong and their defence that they were only 'following orders' was not a justifiable defence.

Ethical theories and jus in bello

A utilitarian might justify war on the basis that it would lead to greater happiness for the greater number, but whose happiness are we taking into account? That of the two nations? That of the victor?

We also need to think about what is moral conduct in war. The principle of utility allows that torture might lead to a greater good, but rule utilitarians might disagree and point to the horrors of Abu Ghraib during the Allied occupation of Iraq as an example of the consequences of allowing the ill treatment of prisoners.

Similarly, utilitarians might disagree over the use of weapons. An act utilitarian might be open to using whichever weapons are most effective, whereas rule utilitarians would ask whether a law restricting some types of weapons, such as chemical or nuclear weapons, might lead to a greater good.

Situation ethics could accept the idea of a just war if it is carried out for the sake of agape. Natural moral law might find some conflict between the primary precepts of preservation of life and an ordered society.

Jus post bellum

Arguably justice, like history, is written by the victors, but just war theorists argue that victory should not provide a licence for imposing harsh measures or allowing commercial interests to dictate the peace. Similarly, imposing an alternative political or religious regime on a country would not be conducive to peace and any programme of rehabilitation imposed by the victors might be superficial and of little long-term

Knowledge check 17

Which of the following are combatants and which non-combatants: a paratrooper, an injured pilot, an army chaplain, a guerrilla fighter, a child soldier?

Knowledge check 18

Give an example of a reason for war that might be acceptable to a situation ethicist.

value. One of the key complaints in post-war Iraq has concerned the administration of rehabilitation programmes which have seemed to favour one ethnic group over another, or further the business interests of private companies. The aim should be to conclude a peace on terms that are not likely to cause further war through bitterness or resentment.

If the defeated aggressors are guilty of atrocities, for example the Nazis or those guilty of ethnic cleansing in the former Yugoslavia, should they be tried as 'war criminals'? Just war theorists argue that any trials should be held in neutral countries with neutral parties presiding and that all atrocities committed in war should be investigated regardless of victory or defeat. So, while we might support the Nuremberg trials of 1945 and 1946, we might also question why no Allied generals or politicians were held accountable for atrocities committed in bombing German towns, or the dropping of nuclear bombs on the Japanese cities of Hiroshima and Nagasaki in 1945.

Evaluating just war theory

The principles of just war theory seem sound. If wars are to be fought then it seems desirable to make some attempt to differentiate just from unjust conflicts and to create criteria by which to judge them. However, modern warfare and modern conflict situations do not make distinctions easy to draw.

The fact that a significant number of nations now have nuclear weapons and other weapons of mass destruction has arguably made the criteria for just war redundant because of the risk they pose and the fact that they lead to indiscriminate killing. On the other hand, governments argue that such weapons serve a useful deterrent function as no one is prepared to use them and risk retaliation.

Finally, we could point to the moral inconsistency of just war theory: justice is about equality and fairness, but war is about winning or losing.

Pacifism

Most pacifists argue that no war can ever be just. They are opposed to violence and conflict on the basis that it is inherently wrong to harm or kill other human beings. This view is consistent with the primary precept of preserving life in natural law.

Christianity and pacifism

Pacifism was a position held by Christians during the Church's first 300 years. Early Christians argued that being a Christian precluded them from becoming a soldier. In part, this was because they would have had to swear allegiance to Caesar, which they felt would imbue him with divine status. Early Christians also felt that using a sword to injure and kill enemy soldiers went against the teachings of Jesus.

Some verses in the Bible suggest that Christ himself was a pacifist. Pacifists argue that Jesus preached and modelled a law of non-resistance, which implies that no war is ever just. This argument is based on the Sermon on the Mount:

> You have heard that it was said, 'An eye for an eye and a tooth for a tooth.' But I say to you, Do not resist the one who is evil. But if anyone slaps you on the right cheek, turn to him the other also.

Matthew 5:38–9

Key quotation

Then Jesus said to him, 'Put your sword back into its place. For all who take the sword will perish by the sword.'

Matthew 26:52

Non-resistance is the practice of not resisting authority, even if it is acting unjustly. It rejects all forms of physical resistance and physical violence exercised by an individual, a group or an institution; it doesn't allow for any form of self-defence and refuses retaliation. This is because we cannot turn to violence to respond to violence. Pacifists feel it is their duty to follow in the footsteps of Jesus: in the same way that Jesus did not retaliate against the violence inflicted on him, we shouldn't resist evil in any circumstance or condition. Pacifists also believe that war is inconsistent with the ethic of love.

It seems, then, that killing an enemy after Jesus sacrificed himself for humankind is morally inconsistent. Not all Christians agree with this view, however. While the Christian argument for pacifism stems essentially from the Sermon on the Mount, others argue that only Jesus, as the redeemer of humanity, can truly argue for pacifism. Christians have a duty to seek peace and justice, but this doesn't necessarily imply turning the other cheek.

Two Christian groups in particular argue for pacifism:

■ Mennonites, a church which grew out of the Protestant Reformation in the early 1500s, refuse to take part in any military action on the grounds that Jesus states we should love our enemies.
■ The Quakers, or the Religious Society of Friends, a Christian movement founded in 1650, are devoted to peaceful principles, which implies a rejection of any form of violence.

Although rooted in Christianity, pacifism became a political movement at the turn of the twentieth century. Conscription was introduced during the First World War under the Military Service Act 1916 because of the high casualty rate on the battlefield. Some men chose to become conscientious objectors and refused to engage in any form of military action because they held to the principle of pacifism; many faced imprisonment and hostility because of their choice.

Pacifism became widespread in the 1920s and 1930s because of the impact of the First World War; war was felt to be a true evil. However, the rise of fascism in Europe led some pacifists to decide that war could sometimes be justified as the lesser of two evils. The argument for pacifism gained further support after the creation of nuclear weapons because of their unprecedented potential for widespread destruction.

Absolute vs relative pacifism

Absolute pacifism argues for a complete and universal rejection of war and conflict. The moral truth that life has inherent value is absolute. War can never be morally justified because it goes against this principle. For absolute pacifists, just war is a contradiction in terms because two wrongs cannot make a right: further conflict cannot be an answer to conflict. Even military action to protect people or in self-defence is immoral. This type of pacifism is associated with the teachings of Jesus, notably the Sermon on the Mount, and with the Indian leader and activist Mahatma Gandhi.

Relative pacifists argue against violence and war but accept that, at times, war is the lesser of two evils. While we should be committed to peace, an absolutist position is too idealistic; commitment to peace has to be contingent on the situation. The physicist Albert Einstein (1879–1955) and the philosopher Bertrand Russell (1872–1970) both argued that the war against Nazi Germany was necessary as surrender to Hitler was the greater evil.

Key quotation

You have heard that it was said, 'You shall love your neighbour and hate your enemy.' But I say to you, Love your enemies and pray for those who persecute you.

Matthew 5:43–4

Key quotation

My pacifism is an instinctive feeling, a feeling that possesses me because the murder of men is disgusting. My attitude is not derived from any intellectual theory but is based on my deepest antipathy to every kind of cruelty and hatred.

Albert Einstein

Active vs selective pacifism

Active pacifism argues for political engagement through campaigns to promote peace. It politicises debates around peace, keeping them in the public arena, contributing to ongoing scholarly debate about war and peace, and leading active campaigns against specific wars.

Selective pacifism is pacifist about certain methods and actions. Selective pacifists might argue, for example, that using weapons of mass destruction would have devastating consequences and would result in a war without winners. Alongside this might be a belief that some wars are justified. Some would argue, of course, that selective pacifism is not really pacifism at all.

Nuclear pacifism

A different type of pacifism has come to the fore since the Second World War. This is nuclear pacifism, which argues that it is morally wrong and unjustifiable for nations to create or hold nuclear weapons. While conventional warfare may be justifiable, nuclear warfare — or the threat of nuclear warfare — is not, because of the scale of possible destruction and the long-term health implications for survivors and future generations.

The bombings of Hiroshima and Nagasaki near the end of the Second World War, which levelled the two cities, marked a turning point in modern warfare and led to a nuclear arms race between the USA and the USSR. By the 1970s each of the two superpowers had enough nuclear weapons to destroy the other.

Nuclear warfare seems incompatible with the principles of just war. Its logical conclusion is the destruction of civilisation because a nation under nuclear attack would probably retaliate in kind, if it had nuclear capability. It also creates an imbalance of power between nations that have nuclear weapons and those that haven't. On the other hand, there are those who argue for deterrence: nations that have nuclear weapons understand their devastating effect and so are never likely to use them for fear of retaliation, thus maintaining the status quo.

The Campaign for Nuclear Disarmament (CND) is an example of a pressure group which advocates pacifism. It has been at the forefront of campaigns to stop nuclear proliferation through nations with nuclear weapons developing further weapons, or new nations joining the nuclear 'club'. CND advocates unilateral nuclear disarmament as well as non-proliferation. You are probably familiar with the CND symbol, designed by Gerald Holtom in 1958. CND argues that the development and potential use of nuclear weapons can never be justified because of their capacity for mass destruction and the fact that such weapons do not discriminate between civilians and combatants.

Arguments against pacifism

Pacifism is unlikely to become a national policy because it could potentially make a nation vulnerable to attack. The European Economic Community (precursor of the European Union) was created in 1956, a few years after the Second World War, because member states wanted to guarantee that no such war would ever take place again on European soil. This has not prevented the UK from being at war with other

Exam tip

In your exam answers, distinguish clearly between different types of pacifism and explain their rationale.

Knowledge check 19

Is just war possible in the nuclear age? Write down one argument for and one argument against.

countries outside of Europe. Pacifism is dependent on other nations, especially the ones we may be in dispute with, also having a policy of pacifism. In practice, this is unlikely. International agreements through the United Nations (UN) have, however, cemented many countries' dedication to seeking peaceful resolution to conflict.

We can also make a logical case against pacifism. Being a citizen implies enjoying the benefits the state brings, but it also implies having certain duties and responsibilities towards it. Not taking part in war, especially in self-defence, means to fail in an important moral obligation. Arguably, therefore, pacifism is at odds with the concept of citizenship.

Finally, it could be argued that pacifism — especially in its absolute form — is too idealistic in today's world: non-violence simply doesn't work in the face of extreme evil.

> **Exam tip**
>
> When answering evaluative questions, present a balance of arguments, then come to a clear judgement in your conclusion. For example, decide whether it is possible for any war to be just or not.

War and peace: summary

- Augustine and Aquinas argue that some wars can be just if they meet certain criteria.
- *Jus ad bellum* refers to what justifies a war: it must have a rightful cause, be decided based on the correct intention, be declared by a rightful authority and be the last resort. It must also have a reasonable chance of success.
- There must also be rightful conduct in war — *jus in bello*. War must discriminate between combatants and non-combatants, be proportionate and be responsible in its methods.
- Modern theorists have also considered the conduct of states after war and the moral responsibilities the winning side has towards the state or people it has fought against.
- Absolute pacifists claim that no war can ever be just because war goes against the basic principle that all lives have value.
- Relative and selective pacifists disagree with the principles of war and argue that no war can really be just. However, they accept that, in some situations, war is unavoidable and the lesser of two evils. Many saw the rise of Hitler as just such a situation.

Sexual ethics

Attitudes towards sex outside marriage, homosexuality, transsexuality, masturbation, divorce and contraception have changed dramatically in the last 60 years or so. The sexual liberation of the 1960s has meant that religious teachings about sexuality and sexual behaviour may appear to have become redundant. However, while culture, tradition and societal norms play a role in how we make decisions about our sexuality, religion still has value. Religion makes us think about what the purpose of sex is and how we can establish meaningful relationships with others. The key question, though, is whether religious perspectives are compatible with modern, liberal attitudes to sex.

Peter Vardy: *The Puzzle of Sex*

In *The Puzzle of Sex*, Vardy outlines the history of our attitudes to sex from a philosophical and religious perspective and argues that the link between sex and reproduction has been broken. He identifies key areas of concern or challenge in modern attitudes to sex and points to inconsistencies in our thinking.

- Under-age sex is considered morally wrong in the UK and the legal age of consent is set at 16; outside the UK, however, this age varies between 13 and 18. Indeed, in some countries, a girl can get married as soon as she reaches puberty, which could be as early as 10. While **adultery** is considered morally wrong but not a crime in the Western world, it is a crime in some nations. Similarly, **pre-marital sex** and homosexuality are crimes in some nations but not in the Western world. What this shows is that attitudes to sex and sexuality are not absolute: it is difficult clearly to determine what is moral or not in relation to sex.

- Vardy is concerned with liberal attitudes to sex whereby any act has become acceptable within the boundaries of consent. He argues that sex has become a commodity legitimised by science and encouraged by mass media. The purpose of sex has become enjoyment rather than divine union: its status as an act of love, even a sacred act for some, has been lost. Vardy also makes a link between liberal, tolerant attitudes to sex, which for him includes pornography and internet sex, and the declining rate of marriage and increase in divorce.

> **Adultery** Sex with someone other than your marriage partner.
>
> **Pre-marital sex** Sex before marriage.

Key thinker
Peter Vardy (b.1945) Vardy is a British theologian and specialist in the philosophy of Kierkegaard who has written extensively about religion and ethics. From 1999 to 2011 he was vice-principal of Heythrop College, a university college in London originally founded by the Jesuits. He now runs A-level religious conferences throughout the UK. He published *The Puzzle of Sex* in 1997.

Many of us may disagree with Vardy but he raises key questions:
- Should religion concern itself with sexual choices?
- Have modern lifestyles and choices meant that religions have had to adapt themselves to new approaches to sexuality?

Christian approaches to sexual ethics

Biblical teachings on sex

The Old Testament includes moving love stories such as the story of Ruth, who has lost her husband and marries Boaz, an older man who has shown her great kindness. It also includes detailed accounts of incest, such as the story of Lot and his daughters in Genesis 19, as well as numerous tales of seduction and sexual revenge — and a celebratory hymn to sex in the Song of Songs.

In Genesis 1 and 2 there is an understanding that sex is a good thing created by God and meant for procreation. However, there are guidelines:

> **Exam tip**
>
> As part of your exam preparation, learn some short quotes to use in your answers.

- Sexual involvement with non-Israelites was forbidden, as it would lead away from God — shown by the story of Solomon and his 700 wives and 300 concubines (1 Kings 11:1–13).
- Adultery was regarded as theft and so punishable by stoning.
- Women should be virgins on marriage, so that the man could be certain that any children were his own.

In the New Testament, Jesus says very little about sex; in fact he gave very few rules and instructions, but called on his followers to live as part of the Kingdom of God, to reflect God's love for all people through the lives they led, and to live justly with one another.

St Paul, who is considered the author of the First Epistle to the Corinthians in the New Testament and who was influenced by Greek thinking, attempted to move the Christian people away from the body towards the soul and appears to take a firmer line:

> Flee from sexual immorality. Every other sin a person commits is outside the body, but he who sins sexually sins against his own body. Or do you not know that your body is a temple of the Holy Spirit within you, whom you have from God? You are not your own.

St Paul (1 Corinthians 6:18–9)

Paul compares marriage to the relationship between Christ and his Church: the man is the head of the household as Christ is head of the Church.

Of course, biblical teachings on sex, and much else, reflect the culture within which they were written and we should not necessarily take them at face value; they require careful interpretation.

Church teachings on sex

Early Christianity (up to 325 CE) valued celibacy because it modelled the life Jesus had chosen and was a gift from God to the priesthood. This is a position still held by the Roman Catholic Church, whose priests, monks and nuns cannot marry or engage in any sexual relationship. Early Christian theologians such as Augustine portrayed sex to be immoral and sinful except for the purposes of reproduction to populate the human race. This view was based upon the Genesis account of God giving man the instruction to go forth and multiply on Earth.

Today, three main views dominate:

- sex for procreation within heterosexual marriage — broadly the Roman Catholic view
- sex within marriage, but not necessarily for procreation — broadly the evangelical Christian view
- sex as an expression of a loving, committed relationship — broadly the liberal Christian view

Roman Catholicism

Roman Catholicism's views on sexual ethics stem from the natural law of Aquinas and its primary precepts of preserving life, procreation and an ordered society.

Key quotation

The body is not meant for sexual immorality, but for the Lord, and the Lord for the body.

St Paul (1 Corinthians 6:13)

Key quotation

Therefore a man shall leave his father and mother and hold fast to his wife, and the two shall become one flesh. This mystery is profound, and I am saying that it refers to Christ and the church.

St Paul (Ephesians 5:31–2)

Roman Catholics therefore believe that the purpose of marriage is procreation and, because society must be ordered, anything that threatens the institution of family and marriage is wrong. Sex is moral only within the boundaries of marriage and with the sole purpose of reproduction. Pre-marital and extra-marital sex are immoral, as are masturbation, homosexuality, contraception and abortion.

For Roman Catholicism, there are three purposes for marriage: faithfulness (*fides*), reproduction (*proles*) and two people becoming one through divine union (*sacramentum*). Any sexual act which goes against one of those three purposes is wrong. That means divorce is immoral because the union between a man and a woman is sacred and cannot be broken.

Homosexuality

Roman Catholicism argues that sexual inclination towards someone of the same sex is not wrong as long as it is not acted upon; it is a trial, a test from God. Homosexuals must be treated with respect and compassion and the Roman Catholic Church condemns any act of violence or persecution.

Despite this, it argues that homosexuality is immoral, for two main reasons:

- Passages from the Bible condemn homosexuality. St Paul describes people engaging in same-sex sexual acts as 'dishonouring their bodies'; this statement is often cited to justify condemnation of gay relationships.
- Natural law theory argues that the purpose of a sexual relationship is procreation. Any union that cannot physically lead to reproduction is therefore considered immoral.

For Roman Catholicism, then, homosexual practices are immoral because they go against both divine and natural law.

The institution of marriage was created by God as a permanent and sacred union between man and wife and cannot be changed or adapted. This is why the Roman Catholic Church is against gay marriage. For different reasons, the Roman Catholic Church doesn't accept gay ministers.

On the one hand, then, the Roman Catholic Church calls for every human being to be treated equally, and understands that people have different sexual inclinations. On the other hand, it condemns the practice of homosexuality and is against gay marriage, which is at odds with modern liberal views.

Critics of the natural law approach to homosexuality argue that sex has a non-reproductive purpose, the uniting act between a loving couple. Many sexual acts cannot lead to pregnancy: sex during the non-fertile part of the monthly cycle, sex after the menopause, sex when one or both partners are infertile, sex when the woman is already pregnant. If the reproductive imperative in sex is rejected, then the natural law position on homosexual sex no longer holds.

Contraception and infertility

Roman Catholic thinking on reproduction and procreation originates in natural law. The purpose of sexual intercourse is the bearing of children: that means couples should not actively prevent childbearing but should accept the situation when sexual intercourse doesn't lead to procreation.

Exam tip

Many of the topics in this part of the course are contentious. Even if you feel strongly, avoid being dogmatic: justify your reasoning using clear arguments.

Knowledge check 20

What is the purpose of marriage for a Roman Catholic?

The Roman Catholic Church believes that artificial contraception is sinful, whether it is a method that prevents conception (e.g. a condom) or a method that induces an early abortion (e.g. the morning-after pill). In the latter case this is because, for Roman Catholics, life begins at conception and a fertilised egg is a person. Natural family planning is acceptable if the couple feels that they would not be able to raise a child: this means avoiding sexual intercourse at times when a woman may be fertile.

The Roman Catholic Church also feels that using contraception encourages immoral behaviour, specifically pre-marital or extra-marital sex, thus damaging the institution of marriage, reducing male respect for women and giving human beings the idea that they can have complete power over the body.

What about couples who are struggling to conceive? Roman Catholics argue against any artificial means of procreation because children are a gift from God and not a right. Roman Catholicism argues against those methods of procreation for two main reasons:

- If donor eggs or sperm are used, it goes against the unity and integrity of marriage, which is a divine union (*sacramentum*).
- IVF procedures involve the selection of viable embryos which means some embryos are discarded, which equates to killing a human life.

Therefore there can be no moral solution to infertility.

While the Roman Catholic Church gives clear answers to sexual ethical issues, there is concern for the impact this has on relationships and family life. For example, a lack of availability of contraception has contributed to the catastrophic spread of HIV in some African countries and of the Zika virus in South America. Sexual abstinence is not really a practical solution to such problems.

Pope Francis, elected in 2013, accepts birth control in principle, and has stopped calling artificial contraception evil, but favours natural contraception. He has argued that artificial contraception is warranted in order to control Zika virus; in this case, the prevention of pregnancy is morally acceptable. He still argues that abortion is an evil.

Jack Dominian's critique of Roman Catholicism

Through his work in psychiatry, Dominian realised that Catholic teachings on marriage were too absolute and legalistic. He argued that a view of marriage as a sacred bond which cannot be broken could not prevent loveless marriages and marital breakdown, but that religion and psychiatry could work together to support couples.

> **Key thinker**
>
> ### Jack Dominian (1929–2014)
> Jack Dominian was a Roman Catholic clinical psychiatrist and theologian who worked for many years as a consultant for the Catholic Marriage Advisory Council. Although upholding the importance of marriage, he was very critical of his church's view on sex and relationships.

IVF *In vitro* fertilisation, where an egg is combined with sperm outside the body.

Exam tip

Section C of Paper 2 requires you to make synoptic links with other areas of the course. For example, you may need to make connections between sexual ethics and the philosophy of religion or the study of a particular religion.

In *Passionate and Compassionate Love*, Dominian calls for a new definition or description of sex, one that sees sex as a personal expression that communicates recognition and appreciation, confirms sexual identity, brings reconciliation and healing, celebrates life, and is a profound way of thanking one another for a loving partnership.

He argues as follows:

- Marriage reflects God's love but should be a place where partners find love, understanding, kinship and forgiveness. This is also the best place to raise children.
- Couples should be able to access pre-marital counselling; churches have a duty to prepare couples for marriage as well as offering counselling when problems arise.
- The Roman Catholic Church is too hierarchical and similar to the relationship between parent and child. Dominian questions its teachings on a range of ethical issues, including sex before marriage, contraception, homosexuality and masturbation. Human beings are rational enough to choose the most moral thing to do according to their individual circumstances.

In an article called 'High Moral Principles' published in the *New Internationalist* magazine in 1986, Dominian specifically addresses the need for change:

> So 'Should the Church move with the times?' The answer must be 'Yes'. Society has a lot to teach the Church about sex. But Christianity, too, embodies fundamental truths which — although in need of equally fundamental rethinking themselves — carry basic values which society ignores at its peril.

According to Dominian, it is possible to be a Roman Catholic but also accept contraception and homosexuality; what matters is a loving relationship and a nurturing environment. He accepts that the teachings of the Bible condemn homosexual practices, but argues that this should not prevent same-sex marriages and that couples should receive the support of Church and state. Contrary to Roman Catholic teachings, he doesn't see reproduction as the sole purpose of sex. Sexual pleasure for Dominian is a gift from God; if it takes place within a loving relationship, it is moral.

This argument seems more in line with the Liberal Protestant outlook or even with secular approaches. Some Roman Catholics have been deeply critical of Dominian, saying that his views are a perversion of the Bible's message on sexual ethics and go against natural law.

Protestantism

Protestants make up about a third of all Christians and belong to a variety of individual denominations. What these have in common is a view of the Bible as the sole source of infallible truth.

Broadly, the Protestant view is that morality comes from the individual conscience rather than church teachings. Sex is an act which can preserve the institution of marriage and is not solely a means to the end of procreation. Contraception may be necessary to protect the institution of marriage for couples who feel, for example, that they cannot support children. Nowadays most Protestant denominations permit artificial birth control to some extent.

Key quotation

Every time we make love we are in the presence of God.

Jack Dominian

Knowledge check 21

Give at least two ways in which Jack Dominian's view differs from traditional Roman Catholic teachings.

Liberal Protestantism

Liberal Protestantism is an umbrella term for a variety of denominations that share a common belief in God as a universal father, mankind as a brotherhood and the soul as having inherent value rather than being a source of sin. It does not follow natural law and argues that we should not interpret the Bible literally but approach it metaphorically as a body of stories from which we can extract ethical and religious truths.

Liberal Protestantism takes the 'sex within a loving relationship' view and is more accepting of homosexuality, cohabitation and sexual relations outside of marriage than is Roman Catholicism. Love is central to human relationships and sex is an expression of that love.

The situation ethics that Joseph Fletcher advocates (see p. 36) is a form of Liberal Protestantism. Fletcher doesn't reject Christian moral principles, but argues that they should be put aside if they undermine the value of love.

The following positions characterise Liberal Protestantism:

- The quality of a relationship is what determines its moral value. Lifelong homosexual relationships are acceptable. Liberal Protestants dispute the interpretation of certain biblical passages and draw on the teaching that all are made 'in the image and likeness of God'. God created homosexual men and women, so they must be good.
- Divorce is morally acceptable in cases of irreversible marriage breakdown or adultery. Remarriage is permissible. What matters first is agape, reflecting the situation ethics of Robinson and Fletcher.
- With regard to pre-marital sex and cohabitation, the key is once again love, justice and consent.
- Almost all non-Catholic Christians believe that any form of contraception should be allowed as long as it is used to limit the size of the family and not to stop having children altogether. A smaller family is better for women's health and allows for a better standard of living. Sex is for enjoyment and to strengthen a marriage as well as for procreation. It is better to combat HIV by using condoms than to expect everyone to follow Christian rules about sex and marriage.
- IVF and artificial insemination are morally acceptable because such techniques can bring happiness to people who otherwise would not be able to have children. If life comes from God, anything that creates new life must be good. In terms of situation ethics, the most loving action is to offer medical help and to use the God-given gifts of healing.

Is Liberal Protestantism truly a religious view?

Liberal Protestantism faces some of the same criticisms situation ethics had to face.

- On the one hand, Liberal Protestantism refers to key biblical teachings on love and justice and sees the teachings of Jesus as a message of acceptance rather than condemnation.
- On the other hand, as Roman Catholicism argues, it ignores key religious moral laws clearly stated in the Bible. On this view, Liberal Protestantism is too relativistic and justifies what many would regard as immoral.

Evangelical Protestantism

Evangelical Protestantism is not a formal movement, but represents conservative elements from within numerous mainstream Protestant denominations as well as independent Baptist churches and Bible churches.

Evangelical churches have a set of beliefs in common:

- Salvation comes about as the result of God's grace through Christ rather than through human action.
- The scriptures are the only source of authority and inspiration; believers take a literal approach to biblical arguments.
- There is emphasis on the conversion experience, typically referred to as being 'born again' or experiencing a 'new birth'.
- Mission work is an important responsibility for believers.

Marriage and extra-marital sex

Evangelical Christians argue that marriage is a sacred union because the partners become one flesh through marriage. There is an acceptance that sex is for enjoyment as well as procreation but, because the ultimate purpose of sex is procreation, sex should only take place in a heterosexual relationship, within the boundaries of marriage. Children are best raised in a stable family environment and only marriage can provide this stability. However, divorce — the breaking of the divine bond — is sometimes a necessary evil.

Some Evangelical organisations such as True Love Waits and Silver Ring Thing actively campaign for celibacy among teenagers, encouraging them to wait until marriage.

Homosexuality

Many Evangelical Protestants believe that homosexuality is a sin. The Bible explicitly condemns homosexual acts, although the salvation of Christ can remove all sins, including homosexuality. However, homosexuals should be welcomed into the Church just as any other person would be and there should be no tolerance of homophobia.

Some Churches advocate controversial conversion therapy, whereby people with homosexual tendencies or feelings undergo psychological treatment or spiritual counselling designed to change their sexual orientation from homosexual or bisexual to heterosexual. Such treatments have been criticised as a form of pseudoscience. Medical, scientific and government organisations in both the USA and Britain have expressed concern over conversion therapy and consider it potentially harmful. Minors are especially vulnerable, and there is evidence that conversion therapy can lead to depression, anxiety, drug use, homelessness and suicide.

Fertility

There is some consensus that IVF and artificial insemination are acceptable. Evangelical Protestants argue that it is right for scientists to try to learn more about the causes of and cures for infertility. There is acceptance of the use of 'spare' embryos in medical research, but only up to 14 days after fertilisation. All Evangelical churches agree that surrogacy is wrong because it involves a third party in a much more significant way than donated eggs and sperm and can potentially strike at the heart of the family.

Key quotation

If a man lies with a male as with a woman, both of them have committed an abomination; they shall surely be put to death; their blood is upon them.

Leviticus 20:13

Knowledge check 22

Summarise the key differences between Liberal and Evangelical Protestant positions on sexual ethics.

A middle ground?

Overall, Evangelical Protestantism stands somewhere between Catholicism and Liberal Protestantism in its views on sexual ethics. It seems less dogmatic than Catholicism and more flexible with regard to infertility and contraception. There are concerns about its attitude to homosexuality, however, in particular about the conversion therapies advocated by some churches.

Libertarian approaches

See also the Key thinker box on John Stuart Mill in the section on equality (p. 20).

To a great extent, we now live in a libertarian and tolerant society. Contemporary secular attitudes to sex emphasise a contractarian ethic whereby sex is morally permissible if there is mutual agreement or consent between the participating parties. Sex is not linked with marriage or reproduction. Human freedom and autonomy are the most important principles and values.

This view derives from John Stuart Mill's harm principle that an action is morally acceptable if no harm is done to either party or other third parties. 'Harm' here means physical harm or harm to someone's interest. Mill's liberal philosophy stems directly from his utilitarian argument. While Mill argues that we should privilege higher pleasures over lower pleasures, freedom of choice is paramount. Through what he classes as experiments in living, we can determine what actions are better for us. Human beings can only flourish if they have the freedom to pursue their own good in their own way without interference from society or oppressive religious institutions.

Provided that no harm is done to either party or to any third party, there is no restriction on the kind of sexual activity engaged in, no requirement to avoid sexual acts that do not lead to reproduction, and no problem with regard to contraception. This approach celebrates the sexual liberation of the 1960s.

However, libertarian approaches, and by extension hedonistic utilitarianism, can struggle to make a clear distinction between harm and offence. Any consensual act is morally acceptable, but what about pornography or prostitution? These are apparently consensual (although this is open to question in some cases) and may not cause direct harm, but many see them as degrading and there is concern over indirect harms, for example the effect of pornography on young men's attitudes to sex.

Secular (non-religious) thinking is not necessarily libertarian: some conservative secular thinkers argue that a libertarian approach to sex and sexuality can damage society. In 1957, the Wolfenden Report recommended the decriminalisation of homosexuality in England and Wales. This caused a major debate between H. A. L. Hart, professor of jurisprudence at Oxford University, and Lord Devlin, a senior judge:

- Devlin opposed the principle on which the report was based, that there should be an area of private morality which was none of the law's business.
- Hart defended the report using Mill's arguments from *On Liberty*: that the law's function is to preserve public order and decency and to protect against the exploitation and corruption of others, but not to intervene in the private lives of citizens or to enforce a pattern of behaviour.

Libertarian Someone who believes that people should be free to think and behave as they wish without limits imposed by authorities such as governments.

Contractarian ethic A general ethical theory that individuals make the right choices for themselves under some form of social contract.

Key quotation

The only purpose for which power can be rightfully exercised over any member of a civilized community, against his will, is to prevent harm to others.

J. S. Mill

Feminist perspectives

Some feminists criticise both traditional Christian and liberal approaches to sexuality. Christian approaches rest on a defined cultural role for women, that of mother and wife, which feminists consider a submissive role that disempowers women, restricts their status in society and socialises them to meet the desires of men. The Hebrew and Greek view of women has meant that, for centuries, women have had little access to political power or wealth and very little free choice. Sexual behaviour assumes male dominance and female submission — most sexual crimes are committed against women.

Feminists also criticise liberal approaches to sexuality, arguing that these approaches assume a level playing field between the sexes. Feminists argue that women may not be as free as men to enter into sexual relationships owing to their oppression by men.

In *Feminism Unmodified: Discourses on Life and Law* (1987), Catharine MacKinnon (b.1946) argues that moral sexual relationships are not possible until sexuality is reimagined and remade; until this happens, sexual activity is immoral.

Key quotation

Women may be so conditioned that they are not even aware of their disempowered status.

Catharine MacKinnon

Exam tip

As part of your revision, create a revision table or mind map summarising the positions of Roman Catholics, Liberal Protestants, Evangelical Protestants and secular liberals on sexual ethical issues.

Sexual ethics: summary

- Overall, Christian approaches to sex are based on the view that the primary purpose of sex is procreation.
- Roman Catholicism considers any sexual relationship outside marriage as immoral on the basis of natural law. Marriage is a sacred union, and anything that goes against this is immoral; this includes artificial fertility procedures like IVF.
- However, the Catholic theologian Jack Dominian argues that sex is a personal expression of love — we should be able to choose freely who we love. That means homosexual relationships should be allowed, as well as divorce.
- The Evangelical Protestant position is similar to that of Catholicism in that both believe that homosexuals should be welcomed into the Church but that homosexuals should not act on their desires. However, some Evangelical churches advocate controversial conversion therapy, which can be damaging. Most Evangelical churches allow for fertility treatment.
- For Liberal Protestants, the quality of a relationship determines its moral value so homosexuality, cohabitation and sexual relations outside marriage are acceptable within the context of a loving relationship. Love is central to human relationships and sex is an expression of that love.
- Secular liberal approaches are based on the principle of consent and the prevention of harm. Sexual choices are a private matter. However, some feminists argue that liberal approaches still accept male dominance.

■ Ethical language

Meta-ethics

Meta-ethics doesn't attempt to tell us what makes something right or wrong or how to act; that is the focus of **normative ethics**. Meta-ethics analyses the reasoning behind ethical language and moral terms such as 'good' and 'right'.

There are two main views:

■ Cognitivism — moral truths exist independently of our mind. Moral judgements can be true or false; terms such as 'right' and 'wrong' correspond to facts in the world.

■ Non-cognitivism — there is no such thing as moral truth in the world; what we call moral facts are subjective emotional responses.

The fact–value distinction

One of the main concerns of meta-ethics is to understand the relationship between facts and values.

■ A fact is a statement that can be true or false, for example 'There are two people in the room.'

■ A value is a belief, judgement or attitude, for example 'Killing is always wrong.'

The issue is whether a value judgement, such as 'Abortion is wrong', can be considered a fact.

■ Most cognitivists are moral **realists**: they argue that, factually, certain actions are right or wrong. Moral judgements can be objective moral facts — they are based on what the world is, independent of our minds.

■ Non-cognitivists are moral **anti-realists**: they argue that moral facts do not exist. A person making a moral judgement is not describing the way the world is but expressing a value, which is subjective and mind-dependent.

The is–ought gap

> **Key thinker**
>
> ### David Hume (1711–76)
>
> David Hume was a Scottish historian and philosopher. He was a religious sceptic and empiricist who argued that human knowledge is founded on experience. His *Enquiry Concerning Human Understanding* was published in 1748. Hume concluded that arguments about God are futile because those who claim to experience God cannot repeat this experience for others to see. He questioned the validity of inductive reasoning, challenging the notion that we can draw conclusions from a few observations or presuppose that events in the future will always hold true because they have done so in the past.

In his *Treatise of Human Nature*, Hume argued that deriving what *ought* to be done from what *is* the case is an example of false deduction. Non-cognitivists argue that we cannot reason from statements of fact to statements of value. The fact that a foetus

Normative ethics
A category of moral philosophy that explains how we ought to live, what constitutes right conduct and the reasons for good actions. The three main normative theories are utilitarianism, deontological (or Kantian) ethics and virtue theory.

Realist The view that moral properties exist in the world and that there is a moral reality.

Anti-realist The view that there are no moral properties in the world and no moral reality.

feels pain doesn't dictate that women should or shouldn't have an abortion; other factors are relevant. Values are not in the world; they are emotional responses to the world. What we call right and wrong are not properties of objects or events in the world but values we ascribe to them. However, if moral judgements are not factual, non-cognitivism cannot claim that something like rape or genocide is inherently wrong, and it cannot account for moral progress.

Cognitivists, on the other hand, attempt to bridge the gap between 'is' and 'ought' and argue that morality is attached to certain facts and ideas that all people share. We can discover moral truths through reason, experience or intuition. Cognitivists account better for moral truth and moral progress because there is moral knowledge: it is possible to say that slavery, rape and genocide are wrong. However, cognitivists are not always successful in accounting for moral motivation: I might have the moral knowledge that stealing is wrong but do it anyway.

Cognitivism: ethical naturalism

See also the Key thinker box on John Stuart Mill in the section on equality (p. 20).

Naturalism is the view that there are moral properties in the world. It is a cognitivist and realist argument. **Ethical naturalism** is **empiricist** in nature. Our moral judgements are derived from our experience of the world; a moral term, such as 'good', can be understood in natural terms, which means we can explain what the term 'good' means with reference to things that are not moral.

So for naturalists:

- The Good is a natural property of the world. A natural property can be a physical or a psychological feature.
- We can infer from those properties what the Good actually is.

Utilitarianism argues for psychological properties. For J. S. Mill, the utilitarian understanding of human nature and human motivation is the origin of morality:

P1 The end (the aim) of our desires is happiness.

P2 Things are desirable in so far as people desire them in the same way as sounds are audible in so far as people hear them.

P3 Personal happiness is a good to each person.

P4 As society is a sum of individual interests, general happiness is a good for this sum of interests (the principle of utility).

C Therefore, the Good is happiness.

P3 bridges the fact–value distinction. Mill makes the fundamental assumption that pleasure and happiness are the Good and doesn't prove it; it requires no evidence as Mill sees it as self-evident.

When Mill refers to 'the Good', he is referring to morality as a whole. The Good is not something transcendent which we can only work out through reason; it is something derived from our very nature as animals.

Ethical naturalism The argument that 'good' is a natural property in the world that can be discovered empirically.

Empiricism The theory that all knowledge is based on sense-experience.

Key quotation

Pleasure and freedom from pain are the only things that are desirable as ends, and … everything that is desirable at all is so either for the pleasure inherent in it or as means to the promotion of pleasure and the prevention of pain.

J. S. Mill

Strengths of ethical naturalism

- Ethical naturalism accounts for our moral feelings when we feel outraged by a clear injustice: it gives us pain, which makes us unhappy and leads naturally to the fact that it was morally wrong.
- Naturalism also accounts for moral disagreements. If we think about the consequences of our actions in terms of whether they produce pleasure or pain, we can decide what is morally right or wrong.
- Naturalism is an effective cognitivist theory as it explains how we use moral language. When we make moral judgements, we state them as facts and imply that they represent something about the nature of reality. When I say torture is wrong, I am not just saying that torture is painful or that I don't like it, I am implying that the claim that torture is wrong is a fact about the world.
- Naturalism seems to be in line with how most people understand morality. We all value pleasure over pain, so it makes sense to argue that the Good is pleasure.

Problems with ethical naturalism

Naturalism is guilty of reductionism in so far as it limits or reduces moral judgements to natural facts about the world. The fact that we seek happiness does not mean that morality should be reduced to seeking pleasure.

The main problem, however, is that it doesn't distinguish between facts and values, and implies that an 'ought' can be derived from an 'is', i.e. that the fact that something naturally *is* the case means we *ought* to do it.

Moore's criticism of naturalism

G. E. Moore takes a cognitivist position but argues that the Good cannot be reduced to a natural property of the world. Moore is critical of the fact that the naturalist argument focuses on two fundamental assumptions, that:

- the Good can be defined as a natural property — in Mill's case, happiness or pleasure
- it is possible to infer what is moral from such premises

In *Principia Ethica*, Moore criticises Mill's naturalism in two separate but connected arguments: the open question argument and the naturalistic fallacy.

Key thinker

G. E. Moore (1873–1958)

Moore was a British moral philosopher from the analytic philosophical tradition and a professor at the University of Cambridge. He is most famous for his book *Principia Ethica* (1903).

The open question argument

Moore argues that if the Good was indeed pleasure, as Mill suggests, the answer to the question 'Is the Good pleasure?' would be so obvious that it would just require a simple 'yes' or 'no'; in other words, it would be a **closed question**. But we know that any attempt to define the Good is not as simple as that. The fact that we have to think

Closed question A question that only needs a short answer — either 'yes' or 'no' — or an answer derived from a limited range of possibilities.

about it means it is an **open question**, and therefore the Good cannot be understood naturally as pleasure:

P1 According to naturalism, the Good is pleasure.

P2 If P1 is true, then the question 'Is the Good pleasure?' is equivalent to saying 'Is the Good good?' which is a closed question.

P3 However, when I think about whether the Good is pleasure, I have to reflect on this and my intuition is that it is not a simple 'yes' or 'no' answer.

C Therefore, the Good is not pleasure.

Naturalists like Mill argue that (P1) the Good is pleasure; Moore says that this is a circular argument.

The naturalistic fallacy

This leads Moore to argue that any attempt to define goodness leads to what he calls the naturalistic fallacy. This is the mistake made by normative philosophers who have attempted to define the Good.

The naturalistic fallacy is committed when a non-natural object is given natural properties. Natural properties could be physical properties, such as shapes or colours, but also responses, such as pleasure and pain, pleasant or desirable. When people associate the Good with such natural terms, they reduce this key moral term to natural properties. For Moore, goodness and pleasure are two different things. Goodness is not a natural property like colour, and it is not something that has the potential to give pleasure. Self-interest, pleasure and happiness are not moral terms, and it is a mistake for morality to be defined by them and reduced to them.

Cognitivism: ethical non-naturalism (intuitionism)

Moore argues that we know what is good through the process of intuition: we intuitively know what the Good is. In the same way that we couldn't describe 'yellowness' without pointing to or talking about a yellow object, we cannot describe what goodness is because it is a simple or basic concept that has no properties we can break down and analyse.

Moore's theory is cognitivist because for him moral properties exist and are real even though they are not natural properties. Our moral intuitions must be about something, and the language we use when we describe our moral intuitions implies that they are objective.

Problems with Moore's argument

- Moore accuses Mill of producing a circular argument but commits the same fallacy in his own argument. If the Good is an intuition and intuitions are moral, he is saying the Good is moral (or the Good is good).
- Moore argues that we just know what is good; we can't explain why, it is self-evident. What if intuitions conflict? A Nazi soldier may have felt that killing other human beings was wrong, but also felt an inherent sense of duty. Do some intuitions come first?

The most damaging criticisms, however, come from J. L. Mackie.

Open question A question requiring a more developed answer because there are potentially unlimited answers.

Knowledge check 23

Briefly explain Moore's open question argument and the naturalistic fallacy.

Content Guidance

Mackie: moral values are relative

> ### Key thinker
>
> ### J. L. Mackie (1917–81)
> Mackie was an Australian philosopher who made important contributions to the philosophy of religion, metaphysics and language. He is most famous for *Ethics: Inventing Right and Wrong* (1977). In 1955 he wrote the essay 'Evil and Omnipotence' in which he proposed that belief in the co-existence of evil and an omnipotent God is irrational.

In *Ethics: Inventing Right and Wrong*, J. L. Mackie argues that moral values are relative rather than absolute. Values, whether moral or aesthetic, 'are not part of the fabric of the world'.

Mackie makes the following points:

- There is a difference between kind and cruel actions, between acts of courage and acts of cowardice.
- It is possible to describe such acts and outline their differences, so acts of courage or cowardice are 'part of the fabric of the world'.
- However, the values we ascribe to such acts are not in the world: we can describe acts of cruelty but the value that they are wrong is not an objective fact.

Mackie is critical of moral realism and the view that there are moral properties in the world, be they natural properties (Mill) or intuitions (Moore). He argues that moral properties cannot be absolute because they are culturally relative — they vary from culture to culture, from society to society and even from individual to individual. For example, polygamy is considered moral in some cultures, but not in others.

Ayer: ethical language is symbolic

> ### Key thinker
>
> ### A. J. Ayer (1910–89)
> A. J. Ayer was a British philosopher who made essential contributions to epistemology, the theory of knowledge. He belonged to the logical positivist movement in philosophy, which sought to ground philosophy in empiricism and science. His book *Language, Truth and Logic* (1936), which he wrote at the age of 25, made him famous thanks to the controversial idea that all principles not based on experience, such as God, are meaningless.

Ayer agrees with Mackie that there is nothing factual about ethical language. Instead he argues that ethical language is symbolic, just like religious language. For example, when we think about the Christian cross, we think about Jesus's sacrifice, and the importance of redemption and atonement in Christianity. The cross represents the Christian faith and is understood by a community of believers: the cross is a religious symbol. Similarly, ethical symbols represent something about how human beings interact with the world. Moral rules are symbols in so far as they establish conventions on how to live. Society understands the ethical convention that killing is wrong — but for Ayer, this is not derived from a factual truth that killing is wrong, but from emotions. It is an emotional response to the world.

Thus, Ayer argues that ethical assertions may be symbolic in that they express moral judgements, but in no way are they facts: they do not describe anything about the world and are thus meaningless:

> The presence of an ethical symbol in a proposition adds nothing to its factual content. Thus if I say to someone, 'You acted wrongly in stealing that money,' I am not stating anything more than if I had simply said, 'You stole that money.'

> In adding that this action is wrong, I am not making any further statement about it. I am simply evincing my moral disapproval of it. It is as if I had said, 'You stole that money,' in a peculiar tone of horror, or written it with the addition of some special exclamation marks.

Non-cognitivism: emotivism

Non-cognitive views of morality are mostly inspired by Hume (see the Key thinker box on p. 64), who argues that we cannot derive moral judgements from what we perceive through our senses. Moral statements do not refer to moral properties in the world, either natural or non-natural (intuitions). Moral statements are neither true nor false. There are no moral truths or facts in the world, therefore there is no possibility of moral knowledge.

The two main non-cognitive moral theories are emotivism and prescriptivism.

For Hume, moral judgements are emotional responses to the external world. We don't see the wrongness of a robbery, we see the events of the robbery; the wrongness comes from our emotional reaction (of disapproval) to it. Values cannot logically be derived from fact.

There could be objective morality in so far as humans have similar preferences, and experience pleasure and pain in the same way. For example, we feel pity for others and we don't like to witness suffering.

Modern emotivism: A. J. Ayer

Hume's version of emotivism was adapted by A. J. Ayer. Ayer was a **logical positivist** who was particularly critical of intuitionism.

Ayer wrote as follows:

> We say that a sentence is factually significant to any given person, if, and only if, he knows how to verify the proposition which it purports to express — that is, if he knows what observations would lead him, under certain conditions, to accept the proposition as being true, or reject it as being false.

What he is describing here is the **verification principle**. The focus of the verification principle is not whether a statement is true, but whether it is meaningful.

For Ayer, when we make a moral judgement, we are merely expressing personal feelings and emotions. Moral judgements simply allow us to share our emotions with others. Moral values and judgements are not based on sense-experience and do not correspond to any physical properties in the world, therefore they are neither true nor false.

Knowledge check 24

Explain the difference between ethical naturalism and ethical non-naturalism (intuitionism).

Logical positivism The belief that language is meaningless unless it can be verified empirically through sense-experience.

Verification principle States that a proposition is meaningful if, and only if, it is either true by definition or empirically verifiable.

Problems with Ayer's emotivism

According to Ayer, rightness and wrongness are emotional add-ons that do not affect the factual claim. What this means, however, is that we can never really morally disagree in the way that we can disagree about facts.

Ayer's response to this is that if we try to clarify the fact, the moral disagreement is solved. If it is a fact that animals don't feel pain, then research performed on them would not affect them emotionally so is morally justifiable. For Ayer, such dilemmas are not moral in nature and can be solved in a purely empirical way.

However, people who defend animal rights would argue that most animals are sentient and even those that are not should still have rights; we cannot detach facts from moral considerations. The view that moral judgements could or should be detached from facts doesn't mean that they are meaningless, as Ayer suggests.

This has led critics of Ayer's emotivism to call it the 'boo-hurrah' ethical theory, in so far as he reduces moral judgements and moral language to feelings of pleasure, displeasure or pain. But moral judgements involve more complex emotions, thoughts and feelings than just approval or disapproval.

Problems with emotivism

- Emotivism relies heavily on the fact–value distinction. If the distinction is wrong, the theory collapses. Cognitivism shows that moral values can be based on fact.
- When we make a moral judgement, we don't necessarily try to influence others. For example, a Muslim could argue that eating pork is wrong without expecting non-Muslims to abide by this view. Emotivism doesn't allow for cultural relativism.
- Emotivism doesn't clearly distinguish between non-moral and moral judgements. For example, saying 'Giving to charity is good' and 'This book is good' are similar in so far as they both express a feeling of approval or pleasure, and both imply that others should like the book or act of charity too. Moral judgements cannot be reduced to subjective feelings and emotions. For example, a debate on the morality of abortion would look at arguments relating to the viability of a foetus and what constitutes a person; this involves rational judgement.
- Linked to this is the problem that emotivism doesn't really account for the specificity of moral language, something that Mackie picks up on in his argument. Moral claims are not like any other claims even though they are emotional reactions. Saying 'Honesty is good' is a very different type of claim from 'Chocolate is good'.
- Emotivism doesn't really account for moral uncertainty, not knowing what to do. Should I allow one person to drown to save five? Why am I unsure, why do I feel guilty? Emotivism doesn't really do justice to the role of reason and moral reasoning.
- Brand Blanshard (1892–1987) gives the example of a rabbit caught in a trap. If morality is essentially the expression of emotions felt when witnessing an event, this would mean that if no one is there to observe the rabbit and its pain, the pain is neither good nor bad. Most people would struggle with this idea.
- If nothing is inherently right or wrong, but a moral statement is just an expression of emotion, there is no moral truth and no possibility of moral progress. Values change, but these are no better or no worse than those that went before. However, when we consider the progress made in women's rights and in attitudes towards LGBTQ persons, we feel society has morally progressed.

Knowledge check 25

How do emotivists such as Hume explain moral judgements?

Knowledge check 26

Why doesn't emotivism account for the possibility of moral progress?

Non-cognitivism: prescriptivism

Key thinker

R. M. Hare (1919–2002)

Hare served in the Royal Artillery during the Second World War and was taken prisoner by the Japanese in 1942. His experiences in Japanese prisoner-of-war camps had a profound impact on his subsequent academic career. He became a noted professor of moral philosophy at Oxford and later at Florida University.

Hare, a non-cognitivist, agrees with emotivists that there is no such thing as a moral fact, but disagrees on what moral values are and what they do. Emotivists argue that the chief concern of moral judgements is to express pleasure or displeasure, and to communicate that feeling to others. However, this fails to take into account the fact that the aim of moral judgements is to guide others, to tell them what they 'ought' to do.

For Hare:

- Moral judgements are action-guiding: they prescribe what to do.
- Moral terms are not descriptive but evaluative: they evaluate experiences and recommend or disapprove of them.
- Moral judgements are meaningful when they can apply to everyone in a similar situation — when they are universal and override other preoccupations that have no moral implications.

Prescriptivism places more emphasis on reason than does emotivism. We use reason and logic to make moral judgements even if the reasoning relies on values being derived from facts.

Universalisability and 'overridingness'

- Hare re-uses a term first used by Kant as part of his normative theory of ethics — 'universalisability'. When we say 'ought', we are saying that the action is not only right for us but for everyone in similar circumstances. Hare takes into account that not everyone is in the same situation, but if the variables are broadly similar, then the line of action should be the same.
- Moral judgements override non-moral judgements. If I hold that stealing is wrong, I wouldn't steal money even if I needed it. The moral principle overrides the non-moral consideration of monetary gain.
- Finally, Hare analyses the word 'good'. If I say something is good, I mean that I choose it and that I recommend its choice to others too. Goodness is not a property we can find in an object: we cannot see, touch or smell the Good. We use certain criteria that allow us to decide whether something is good, but this doesn't define goodness itself. The Good itself is evaluative, which means that it puts a value on the object: we commend it and we choose it, and this is the reason it is good. The commendation is intended to be action-guiding or imperative: it tells us what we ought to do. This is what fills the gap between value and fact.

Exam tip

Make a table to clarify and compare the features of the various meta-ethical theories you have studied.

Problems with prescriptivism

- Prescriptivism doesn't account for a clash of moral principles. For example, someone might believe abortion is wrong, and therefore think that life should be preserved at all costs. But what if a pregnant woman's life is at risk because of the foetus she carries? Clearly, two moral principles clash here. Hare argues that, in such circumstances, one of the moral principles must be abandoned, or the two principles must somehow merge and adapt themselves to the situation. In this case, we could say that abortion is morally right if the mother's life is at risk. Universalisability is still possible, because we could create a principle that relates to any broadly similar situation.

- Although Hare tries to make his principle of universalisability as specific as possible by allowing for broadly similar situations to be considered equivalent, circumstances are never completely the same and each situation is unique.

- Hare doesn't account for rational but 'bad' decisions. I might kill a fly because it annoys me, rather than helping it fly out of the window.

- Hare argues that moral considerations override other types of consideration, but how can we make that decision if we cannot clearly differentiate between moral and non-moral uses of the term 'should'?

Exam tip

For cognitivism, the key problem is the fact–value distinction. For non-cognitivism, it is the issue of moral progress.

Knowledge check 27

Explain why emotivism and prescriptivism are non-cognitivist theories of ethics.

Meta-ethics: summary

- Meta-ethics is a field of moral philosophy that investigates moral language.
- Cognitivism is the view that moral beliefs and judgements can be true or false, and that a moral reality exists to be discovered.
- Moral realists argue against the is–ought gap and the fact–value distinction, in so far as they believe that moral judgements can be true or false and don't merely express likes or dislikes, as anti-realists state.
- Naturalists argue that moral terms such as 'goodness' can be understood in non-moral or naturalistic terms — for example, happiness, pleasure or self-interest.
- Intuitionists reject the naturalist idea that morality can be defined in non-moral terms like pleasure. Moral judgements are based on our intuitions about what the Good is.
- Mackie is critical of naturalism and intuitionism on the grounds that they assume that moral language can describe moral absolutes. Instead, he argues that moral language is subjective and describes values that are relative.
- Non-cognitivism is an anti-realist position which argues that there is no such thing as moral truth in the world.
- Emotivism argues that moral judgements and statements are the expression of emotions. Moral terms such as 'good' or 'right' do not refer to anything in the world and cannot be verified. A. J. Ayer has developed a modern version of emotivism based on logical positivism. Critics have called it the 'boo-hurrah' theory of ethics.
- Prescriptivism argues that moral judgements involve not only an emotion but also a command, as we expect others to agree with us. Although moral values are personal, subjective and based on emotions, they are 'universalisable' in so far as we want others to choose the same values.

The relationship between religion and morality

In *The God Delusion*, Richard Dawkins refers to Abraham's readiness to sacrifice his son Isaac to God (Genesis 22:1–19). For Dawkins, religion doesn't just condone immoral actions, it is opposed to morality.

But what is the link between religion and morality? One of the key questions theologians ask is where morality comes from. Does it come from God, as Aquinas or Augustine claim, or is morality independent of God and religion? Are they even opposed, as Dawkins argues? Ultimately, the question is whether following religious principles makes you moral — and whether religion is a good source of morality.

There are three main positions on the link between religion and morality:

- Theonomous ethics argues that morality stems from a universal source, namely God.
- Autonomous ethics argues that moral decisions are decided by the moral agent — ourselves — independently of religion.
- Heteronomous ethics argues that morality is defined by an external force, be it laws, a religious denomination or cultural norms.

Theonomous ethics

For religious believers, it makes sense to argue that morality comes from God:

- God is the creator of moral goodness; all goodness in the universe comes from an omnibenevolent God.
- God is the source of moral knowledge; we must use reason and our moral intuition to discover what is moral (Aquinas).
- God is our motivation for being and doing the Good; acting morally and following God's commands brings human beings closer to God and allows us to achieve rewards in the afterlife.

Divine command theory is a type of theonomous ethics.

Divine command theory

According to divine command theory, something is good because God wills it and God commands us to do it. All moral truths are God-given. Moral rightness originates with God; all that is morally wrong cannot originate with God and is not God-given. Moral truths are eternal, absolute, universal and unchanging because God himself is unchanging. To be moral is simply to obey God's commands.

Problems with divine command theory

- How can moral truths be eternal and unchanging if different religious communities disagree on what they are? A response to this problem involves making a distinction between weak and strong divine command theory. According to weaker versions, God's commands are applicable within the context of a specific religious community. Thus while some religious communities consider homosexuality a sin, more liberal communities do not. However, this still raises the question as to which point of view is 'right'.

Any modern legal system would have prosecuted Abraham for child abuse, and if he had actually carried through his plan to sacrifice Isaac, we would have convicted him of first-degree murder.

Richard Dawkins

- If to be moral is to follow God's commands, the non-believer has no commands to follow and therefore no moral accountability.
- Divine command ethics is circular: it argues that what is good is what God commands and what God commands is good. So *what* is the Good and *why* is it good?
- Many divine commands seem outdated and arbitrary, telling us to behave in a way that we now deem fundamentally immoral. Consider the following, for instance:

> If there is a betrothed virgin, and a man meets her in the city and lies with her then you shall bring them both out to the gate of that city, and you shall stone them to death with stones, the young woman because she did not cry for help though she was in the city, and the man because he violated his neighbour's wife.

Deuteronomy 22:23–4

Some philosophers have come to the defence of divine command ethics. For example, Philip Quinn (1940–2004) agrees that God 'moves the goalposts' at times but argues that we should accept his commands for that very reason. For example, Exodus 20:15 states that we should not kill, but God revokes this when the Israelites are asked to enter the Promised Land and told to kill: 'save alive nothing that breathes' (Deuteronomy 20:16). Quinn argues that this allows God to adjust moral truths and set moral standards applicable to the context. For Quinn, whatever God commands is moral. We could be critical of this, however, on the basis that it goes against our moral intuition that killing is wrong.

The Euthyphro dilemma

Key thinker

Plato (c.428–c.348 BCE)
The founder of the Academy in Athens, Plato was a pupil of Socrates and the teacher of Aristotle. His real name was Aristocles; Plato was a nickname, meaning 'broad' (perhaps in reference to his broad shoulders or forehead). One of the most important and influential philosophers of the classical world, Plato wrote on a variety of topics including epistemology, aesthetics, politics and ethics. His Euthyphro dilemma is the most significant critique of religious morality.

In Plato's dialogue *Euthyphro*, Socrates asks Euthyphro whether something is morally good because the gods command it or whether the gods command something because it is morally good.

- If God is the source of moral goodness (if what he commands is 'good') then God can make what is good bad.
- If God commands us to do things because they are 'good' this implies that God is conforming to an independent standard of goodness.

This choice poses a real challenge to the concept of the **omnipotent** and **omnibenevolent** God of classical **theism**.

Omnipotent All-powerful.

Omnibenevolent All-good.

Theism The belief that God continues to intervene in the universe.

If God is the source of moral goodness and whatever God wills is — by definition — good, then it doesn't make sense to praise God for his goodness. If God can will anything to be morally good, then he could will us to do unjust acts (e.g. murder) which would run against our moral intuitions but which would be right because God willed them. This would make morality arbitrary, but we don't see morality this way, i.e. as something that can be changed by the will of a particular being.

Option 2 is no less problematic. If God commands things because they are good and God is conforming to some independent morality then this suggests that God is not the creator of all things: there is a standard of things outside his control. This means that God is not omnipotent. If one of God's attributes is omnibenevolence then he is having to conform to a standard of morality in order to fulfil it.

Responses to the Euthyphro dilemma

Responses focus on God's nature: if God is by nature good, it makes sense for him to choose what is good for human beings.

For example, the American Christian philosopher Robert Adams (b.1937) argues that although God may appear, at times, to ask humanity to perform immoral actions (as in the story of Abraham and Isaac), he would not ask us to do things that in the long term would harm us. Any of God's commands is moral, but may appear to us immoral because we are at an epistemic distance from God. Moreover, he argues, while God can do all that is logically possible (because he is omnipotent), there are certain things he does not wish to do (what he feels would go against his benevolent nature).

Autonomous ethics

The view that morality is independent from religion usually starts with criticisms of religious morality and the idea of objectively binding laws. The argument is that we have a sense of conscience and moral obligation which can be accounted for without appealing to the existence of God.

Here we are considering **anti-theist** (e.g. R. A. Sharpe) and **atheist** (e.g. Richard Dawkins) arguments as well as Kant's argument that to be moral is to use reason — although this is not incompatible with a belief in God.

Kant's moral argument

> **Key thinker**
>
> **Immanuel Kant (1724–1804)**
> A German philosopher and one of the most influential thinkers of modern Europe and the late Enlightenment, Kant was born, lived and died in the Prussian city of Königsberg, now part of Russia. Kant's main works were on epistemology (the theory of knowledge) and metaphysics (the essence of being). In 1781, he produced his *Critique of Pure Reason*, widely regarded as one of the greatest books on philosophy ever written.

Knowledge check 28
Briefly explain the Euthyphro dilemma.

Anti-theism Direct opposition to the belief in any deity, the argument that theism is harmful to the believer.

Atheism Denial of the existence of God.

Kant's argument is a form of autonomous ethics in that he argues that human beings are rational beings who can discover the moral rule through reason. However, Kant doesn't deny the existence of God and argues that, if God exists, he and humanity abide by the same rational principles.

- Kant's basic premise is that humanity ought to strive towards moral perfection. He argues that human beings have a **good will**: this is the only correct moral intention. A good person is one who acts out of good will and does their duty.
- To act out of good will is to seek to achieve the Highest Good, the *summum bonum*. It follows that this must be achievable: 'ought' implies 'can'.
- However, it is not within our power as humans to achieve it because, although we can strive towards virtue, we cannot ensure that we get what we deserve for our efforts, because we are not omnipotent.
- There must be a rational moral being who, as creator and ruler of the world, has the power to bring moral worth and happiness together.
- As this reward for happiness does not happen in this life, where sometimes the good have lives of tragedy and the wicked prosper, it must be attained in an afterlife.

Kant is aware that this argument doesn't really work as a proof that God exists for unbelievers. However, what is clear to him is that we are moral beings with a sense of duty and that we ought to do something on the basis that it is possible. His conclusion is that we should believe in God because of morality, not logic.

Sharpe's moral case against religious belief

> **Key thinker**
>
> ### R. A. Sharpe (1935–2006)
> Sharpe was a British philosopher who wrote extensively on aesthetics (the philosophy of art) and had a particular interest in the philosophy of music. He was brought up a Baptist but became deeply critical of religious beliefs and their influence on morality.

Sharpe argues that we can make a moral case against religious belief. We need to make a clear distinction between morality and religion. This is because religious institutions have no necessary authority on moral matters; to be religious, or to have religious beliefs, doesn't necessarily entail being moral, or abiding by moral commands. Religions can get it wrong. Furthermore, people follow religious guidelines for their own sake rather than for the sake of being moral.

Sharpe's examples focus on the Roman Catholic Church. In his view, the Catholic Church considers practices to be immoral which, for Sharpe, are not immoral. For example, Paul VI's encyclical unequivocally states that the use of artificial contraception is gravely immoral, even within marriage. Sharpe asks the question, 'Is it remotely conceivable that God should be interested in whether people use a condom rather than the rhythm method of contraception?'

Some religious groups take an even more extreme position on sexual ethics than the Roman Catholic Church.

Good will The motive behind the action, seen by Kant as the source of moral worth, the only good thing.

Key quotation

All our knowledge begins with the senses, proceeds then to the understanding, and ends with reason. There is nothing higher than reason.

Immanuel Kant

Key quotation

Morality is not the doctrine of how we may make ourselves happy, but how we may make ourselves worthy of happiness.

Immanuel Kant

The Westboro Baptist Church

The Westboro Baptist Church is an American hate group founded by Fred Phelps in 1955. They argue that events such as 9/11 and natural disasters are divine retribution for America's support and tolerance of homosexuality. Famous for their slogan 'God hates fags' (which their website describes as 'a profound theological statement, which the world needs to hear more than it needs oxygen, water and bread'), they picket and hold demonstrations at the funerals of soldiers who have been killed abroad, or in front of restaurants which employ gay people.

The group strongly believes in God's wrath and hatred of homosexuals. They support their view using selected quotes from the Bible. The group argues that God only chooses a few communities to be saved and that most people will go to hell. Indeed, their website includes a counter for the number of people who will have gone to hell since the viewer opened their page! The group has a very limited following but has relied on negative publicity, outrageous claims and demonstrations to become notorious.

The Quiverfull movement

This conservative Evangelical Christian religious group stands against artificial contraception and abortion. The movement believes that having children is a blessing from God and that the purpose of sex is reproduction. They therefore argue that any attempt at family planning, whether natural or artificial, is evil. They believe that it is a Christian duty to have as many children as possible to build an 'army of God'. God would not give them more children than they can cope with and so they leave it to God to plan their family.

The movement is inherently patriarchal: women are defined by the fact that they have a womb and can bear children. Nancy Campbell, who runs a website called Above Rubies, argues that the very term 'woman' means 'womb man'. The woman's role is to mother and nurture children, even into adulthood. For a true believer, dying in childbirth is a noble act.

Dawkins: religion is opposed to morality

In his 2006 documentary *The Root of All Evil?*, Dawkins argues that humanity would be better off without religion or belief in God. He argues that religious positions on morality, especially when taught to children, represent a form of indoctrination, teaching dubious and uncritical moral codes. Children who doubt or reject those beliefs are scared with visions of hellfire and eternal damnation.

Key thinker

Richard Dawkins (b.1941)
Richard Dawkins began his career as an evolutionary biologist. His 1976 book *The Selfish Gene* popularised his gene-centred view of evolution. Dawkins is a well-known critic of religious faith and has written numerous books and articles and given many lectures arguing for the use of reason in interpreting the world as opposed to religious faith. He argues that the scientific theory of evolution means that belief in God has become redundant. He is an atheist thinker who sees religious beliefs and practices as child-like and dangerous. His 2006 book *The God Delusion* became a best-seller.

Key quotation

Behold, children are a heritage from the Lord, the fruit of the womb a reward. Like arrows in the hand of a warrior are the children of one's youth. How joyful is the man whose quiver is full of them!

Psalm 127:3–5

Knowledge check 29

How do the beliefs of organisations like the Westboro Baptist Church and Quiverfull support Sharpe's argument?

Religious believers follow the moral codes imposed on them, not for their own sake or because they are the best possible choice but for fear of punishment. Believers 'suck up' to God.

Dawkins advocates a morality based on reason, which values autonomy. Dawkins would like to see a secular, relativist and consequentialist ethics. However, Dawkins' main argument is that moral choices are motivated by evolution. Selfless activity and working with others happens because it has helped organisms to survive. We are moral because it allows us to be successful, survive and reproduce. We can understand morality without God.

Many of Dawkins' examples relate to groups with extreme views. He gives the example of 'hell houses', haunted house-type attractions where American fundamentalist Christians depict sins and the consequences of being immoral to convince patrons to adopt a strict Christian moral life. Children come away traumatised, fearful of divine punishment and brainwashed into thinking that homosexuality, for example, is evil. For Dawkins, this is a form of child abuse. Dawkins calls this 'biblical parenting': condemning some behaviours — masturbation, sex before marriage, homosexuality — as impure to the point where it could lead you to hell.

Dawkins is also very critical of Islam, especially radical Islam and the problem of women's rights in some Muslim countries. In Saudi Arabia, for example, women cannot work or hold a bank account without their father's or husband's permission. Dawkins argues that religions such as Islam condone immoral actions, such as stoning adulterers and chopping off robbers' hands, while advocating backward-looking moral codes which are intolerant and unjust.

Dawkins on terrorism

Dawkins has been widely criticised for generalising from the actions of a few to a whole religion, especially for his comments associating violence with Islam following the 2015 *Charlie Hebdo* terrorist attack in Paris (when French journalists working for the satirical newspaper were killed by Islamist terrorists). While he argues that he is not an Islamophobe, Dawkins has made numerous comments about Muslims suffering because of their religion, which he sees as cruel.

For Dawkins, religion — not just Islam — can be a huge motivator for terrorism. Religious extremism has overtaken national separatism to become the main driver of terrorist attacks around the world. Religious terrorists and violent extremists interpret religion in a way that justifies violence over the peaceful messages of their religion.

Dawkins also feels that religious people abide by these moral codes because they want to score points in heaven and that this way of thinking has been at the root of some terrorist actions: terrorists and radical Islamists often feel that they are God's beloved and that they will be the first to be rewarded in heaven.

Critiques of Dawkins

- Dawkins ignores the role of religion as a force for good. Many religious men and women, clergy included, have made tremendous contributions to humanity in times of war, famine and poverty, and religious activism has been a driving force for peace.
- Dawkins assumes that religious morality is stuck in the past and is not evolving. Many religious beliefs on moral issues are changing over time, albeit slowly.

Key quotation

The God of the Old Testament is arguably the most unpleasant character in all fiction: jealous and proud of it; a petty, unjust, unforgiving control-freak; a vindictive, bloodthirsty ethnic cleanser; a misogynistic, homophobic, racist, infanticidal, genocidal, filicidal, pestilential, megalomaniacal, sadomasochistic, capriciously malevolent bully.

Richard Dawkins

- Dawkins is very selective in his examples, focusing on religious extremism, be it Christian or Muslim, and generalising this to all religion.
- Dawkins ignores the fact that many believers are obedient to God out of love, loyalty and respect, and a desire to be more virtuous, not just because they want to go to heaven.

The relationship between religion and morality: summary

- There are three main positions on the link between religion and morality: theonomy, autonomy and heteronomy.
- Theonomous ethics assumes that morality is dependent on religion.
- Divine command theory argues that to be moral is to obey God's commands. However, God's commands seem arbitrary at times.
- Plato uses the Euthyphro dilemma to demonstrate that God cannot be simultaneously omnibenevolent and omnipotent. This has been one of the keystones of criticisms of religious morality.
- Autonomous views of ethics argue, as Kant does, that morality is first grounded in human reason. For Kant, this doesn't conflict with religious belief.
- Thinkers such as R. A. Sharpe and Richard Dawkins have been much more critical of the link between morality and religion, arguing that religion condemns actions which are not widely considered immoral and, in some cases, promotes behaviour that many people would regard as immoral. Both thinkers are very specific in their choices of examples, however.

■ Deontology, virtue ethics and the works of scholars

A comparison of the work of Immanuel Kant and Aristotle

Concerned about religious intolerance in Europe, but also about uncritical religious dogmatism which focuses on faith rather than reason, Kant sought to create a moral system independent of religion. Kant's approach to ethics is based on the two key ideas of reason and duty, which together form a consistent **deontological** system (see p. 38 for a definition of 'deontological').

Aristotelian virtue ethics judges the person committing the act rather than the act itself. It is an 'agent-centred' form of ethics rather than an 'act-centred' theory like utilitarianism and Kantian ethics. Virtue ethics does not ask 'What have you done?' but 'What kind of person are you?'.

Kantian deontology

See also the Key thinker box on Immanuel Kant in the section on the relationship between religion and morality (p. 75).

Kant argued that morality is independent of God's and everyone else's will: it is part of the fabric of the universe and something we can all discover through reason. We have a sense of moral duty — we feel we know what is right and wrong, and feel compelled to choose what is right.

The good will

Kant believed that the consequences of any action are no guide at all as to the morality of that action. What counts is solely the motive behind the action — the good will.

The good will is free from self-interest or calculation of consequences. It is not about pleasurable emotions such as kindness, because they are to do with personal desires. The good will is in acting solely because it is the right thing to do, it is your duty, and our judgements of the good will are determined by reason alone.

But how do we know which acts it is our moral duty to perform?

The categorical imperative

The word 'imperative' here means 'command'. Kant identifies two types:

■ Hypothetical imperatives depend on you; they are commands that are true only in certain situations — 'If you want x to happen, then you should do y'. Hypothetical imperatives can be abandoned if you no longer will a particular end. They are subject to change and because of this they can never be moral imperatives.

■ Categorical imperatives just say 'Do this'. They embody our moral duty, are unconditionally binding and apply equally to all rational beings. The categorical imperative is universal and necessary rather than subjective and contingent, so we can use it to work out laws that it is our duty to perform.

Kant put forward three formulations of the categorical imperative, two of which will be discussed here.

Virtue ethics An ethical theory that locates moral value in the agent performing the action. It emphasises the need to develop a virtuous disposition and to judge actions in a broader context using practical wisdom.

Exam tip

Kant's *Groundwork for the Metaphysics of Morals* and Aristotle's *Nicomachean Ethics* are both prescribed anthology texts. Use this link to access the *Anthology*:

Section B of Paper 2 will consist of a two-part question on an excerpt from an anthology text.

Contingent Dependent on circumstances.

The first formulation

The first formulation is the principle of universalisability. Would you like the rule you are following to be true for all people, in all cultures, over all time? This is similar to the maxim 'Treat others as you would like to be treated'.

Kant wants to make the rules that we live by objective. He is trying to create a rule that forces us to consider whether what we want to do is right or wrong generally and objectively, rather than based on our experiences or a particular situation.

Kant devised two tests to help us analyse whether the maxims we are thinking of creating are universalisable:

- Contradiction in conception or contradiction in nature — a maxim is wrong if the situation in which everyone acted on that maxim is somehow self-contradictory. The maxim 'Whenever I need money I will borrow some on the promise that I will pay it back, even though I don't intend to' could not be universalised because if everyone borrowed money on a false promise then no one would lend money.
- Contradiction in will — it would be unpleasant to will 'not to help others in need', but it is not self-contradictory. However, it is a contradiction in will because to will the ends (no one helping) one must will the means — but it may be that the only way we can achieve our ends is through help, so we can't will a situation where no one helps us as we would not be able to will the means to our end and we couldn't achieve anything. In willing 'not to help others in need' we are willing contradictory states of affairs.

The second formulation

The second formulation asks us to respect humanity. To treat someone's humanity simply as a means is to treat the person in a way that undermines their power of making a rational choice themselves. Because we are rational beings we have inherent value — we are ends in ourselves and count equally with one another.

The way to treat someone as an end is to consider their feelings and their needs and wants. For example, you should be kind to them because you care about them and want them to be happy. Again, this is similar to the rule 'Treat others as you would like to be treated'. Kant is not saying we should never treat people as a means, but that we should not *only* treat them as means.

Strengths and weaknesses of Kant's argument

Strengths

- Kantian ethics takes account of justice: the innocent man could not be tried and found guilty just because this would benefit the majority. Justice towards the individual is safeguarded by universalisability; we could not will 'Try to find an innocent man guilty' into universal law. For Kant, a human is a being of intrinsic worth, a rational creature and not something to be exploited for the greater happiness of others.
- Kant makes a sharp distinction between duty and inclination, preventing us from assuming that what is good for us is good for everyone else. People of good will obey laws that are the same for all and, in this way, we subordinate our natural inclinations and become more appreciative of the rights of others.

Key quotation

The categorical imperative is thus only a single one, and specifically this: Act only in accordance with that maxim through which you can at the same time will that it become a universal law.

Immanuel Kant

Exam tip

When you write about the categorical imperative, give an example to show how it works.

Key quotation

Always recognise that human individuals are ends and do not use them as a means to your end.

Immanuel Kant

- Kant uses objective reason for the basis of his argument, which demands consistency and necessity. The moral authority for the categorical imperative does not come from God but from us and this gives everyone the means to create a set of moral standards regardless of consequence or circumstance. Kant's argument is strong on human dignity and human rights.

Weaknesses

- There could be a rule that whenever anyone buys a new book they must write their name in it. The fact that a rule can be universalised does not guarantee that it will be morally good, or even moral. Kant argues that we should universalise only those rules that have to do with morality.
- Kant bases his theory on the rationality of human beings. While humans are rational, they do not all have the same temperaments or desires, and therefore different people find different situations tolerable or intolerable. A sadist might wish to universalise sadism.
- Kant's argument creates absolute rules. Most of us would argue that sometimes there are exceptions and that exceptions can be morally permissible. Furthermore, Kant does not make it clear what to do if moral duties conflict.
- For Kant, the good will is the only motive that has moral worth. If someone acts out of sympathy for someone or out of love for a friend or family member, then their action has no moral worth. Kant would argue that he is not asking us not to consider our feelings, only that, when we come to choose, our feelings should not decide the matter.

Overall, Kantian ethics feel too rigid for modern tastes.

Knowledge check 30

Explain the difference between the first and second formulations of the categorical imperative.

Exam tip

An understanding of the strengths and weaknesses of Kantian deontology and Aristotle's virtue ethics is essential to an effective comparison of the two theories.

Is Kant compatible with religious approaches to ethics?

Kant argues that while the good will is the only correct moral intention, to act out of good will is eventually to achieve the Highest Good or *summum bonum*, which is a combination of virtue and happiness. The *summum bonum* is not the *reason* for being moral; rather, it is the later goal *as a result of* being moral.

The *summum bonum* is only attained if we are both moral and happy. By being moral, we should ideally also be happy. Happiness for Kant is quite different from the hedonistic pleasure of the utilitarian. It is grounded in a sense of fulfilment or accomplishment at doing your duty.

However, in many cases, the moral person is exploited and/or never receives their dues. Kant argues that because the *summum bonum* is not often achieved in this life, immortality of the soul and God must exist in order for the *summum bonum* to be achieved after we die. In this way, Kant's deontology is compatible with a religious approach to ethics.

Exam tip

The *summum bonum* is a useful synoptic link between religion and ethics and the study of religion.

W. D. Ross's deontology

Ross was very critical of ethical egoism (the view that we should do what is in our self-interest) and argued that morality should be grounded in our moral intuitions — what we think is right in itself — and in a sense of moral obligation. Ross explains why we regard certain courses of action as good with reference to *prima facie* duties or *prima facie* obligations.

> **Key thinker**
>
> ## William David Ross (1877–1971)
> Ross was a Scottish philosopher who argued for a form of deontological ethics focused on intuition, in response to G. E. Moore's utilitarian take on intuitionism. He is also famous for his translation of Aristotle's works into English.

A *prima facie* duty is a duty that is binding, all other things being equal — that is, unless it is overridden or trumped by another duty or duties. An example of a *prima facie* duty is the duty to keep promises: unless stronger moral considerations override, we ought to keep a promise made.

Ross gives seven examples of *prima facie* duties:

- fidelity — for example, not breaking a promise
- reparation — making amends to people you hurt in the past
- gratitude — being grateful for something someone has done for us, from a simple 'thank you' to returning a favour
- justice and fairness — sharing things fairly
- beneficence — thinking about the wellbeing of others
- self-improvement — trying to be the best kind of person we can be
- non-malfeasance — not purposefully harming others

Ross argues that some moral judgements are so self-evident that they are *prima facie*.

Criticisms of Ross's ethical argument

- How do we know which duties apply in which cases? On what basis has Ross chosen those specific seven duties? Ross argues that these duties are *prima facie* and that we know them intuitively.
- The duties Ross calls *prima facie* might not be derived from intuition but from society's values and our specific upbringing. We do something because it is the norm, not because it is our duty.
- Ross does not explain why we have moral intuitions in the first place. He just assumes that they exist, and does not explain how we distinguish between right and wrong.
- Ross seems to suggest that moral truths are self-evident. However, the fact that we have moral disagreements suggests that morality is not as self-evident as intuitionists suggest.

Thomas Nagel's deontology

For Nagel, the central question in ethics is the reasoning behind our moral choices. He makes a distinction between agent-relative and agent-neutral reasons:

- Agent-relative reasons stem from personal desires, commitments and projects.
- Agent-neutral reasons consider everyone, not just the moral agent making the choice. They are impersonal and objective.

For Nagel, consequentialism — and therefore utilitarianism — is agent-neutral: it is an act-centred ethics as opposed to an agent-centred ethics. For this reason, it is in conflict with common sense. Moral decision-making should be on the basis of agent-relative reasons, which include deontological reasons.

> **Exam tip**
>
> When you write about an ethical theory, consider whether modern philosophers have overcome problems with the theory.

> **Knowledge check 31**
>
> Explain the difference between Nagel's agent-neutral and agent-relative reasons.

> **Key thinker**
>
> ### Thomas Nagel (b.1937)
> Born in Belgrade, Serbia, Nagel is an American philosopher with particular interest in philosophy of mind, ethics and political philosophy.

Agent-relative reasons are:

- reasons of autonomy: choices based on projects, desires and interests; such reasons don't have value for others
- deontological reasons: reasons not to maltreat others; personal demands which limit and govern relations with others
- reasons of obligation: special obligations I have towards people I am close to

The belief that lying or that breaking a promise is wrong involves a deontological reason. This is because I do not want to treat others as a means to an end and I do not want to violate people's rights.

Philosophers have questioned Nagel's distinction. Do agent-neutral reasons actually exist? Is utilitarianism really agent-neutral, considering its basis is pleasure and self-interest, even though I may have to sacrifice that for the sake of the majority?

Aristotelian virtue ethics

See also the Key thinker box on Aristotle in the section on natural moral law (p. 41).

Aristotle gave the first systematic expression to virtue theory in his *Nicomachean Ethics* (350 BCE). Aristotle believed that it is one thing to know 'the Good', but another thing to act on that good.

The function argument

Aristotle thought that anything that a person does has a purpose (*telos*) and a higher aim — it is a rational activity. Aristotle described this as 'the Good' — good for yourself and good for everyone. Everything has a function (*ergon*) and being good is to perform your function well. The end of human action is flourishing and, according to Aristotle, you can truly flourish only when you perform your function well. Every action is a means to that end.

The function argument works as follows:

P1 The Good for members of a kind is to perform well the function distinctive of their kind.

P2 To perform the function distinctive of one's kind well is to perform it in accordance with the relevant virtues.

IC1 Therefore, the Good for members of any kind is to perform their distinctive function in accord with the relevant virtues.

P3 The function distinctive of humans is rationality.

IC2 Therefore, the Good for humans is rationality in accord with virtue.

P4 Happiness is good for humans.

C Therefore, happiness is rationality in accord with virtue.

telos purpose

ergon function

> **Exam tip**
>
> Make use of the Greek terms used in virtue theory if you can, as this will show the examiner that you have a strong grasp of the theory.

> **Exam tip**
>
> You can increase the sophistication of your arguments by including intermediate conclusions (IC) that you arrive at on your way to the main conclusion (C).

The distinctive end purpose of human beings is to be rational, which seems straightforward. However, what is frequently missed is the significance of *ergon* — putting reason into practice. This is where virtue ethics comes into its own. Through the practice (habituation) of *arête* (excellence, therefore virtue), reason becomes an activity of the soul, leading to *eudaimonia* — often translated as 'human flourishing' or 'happiness'. True happiness is the process of flourishing, the joy of being what you are meant to be and doing what you are meant to do and doing it well. This is the *eudaimon* life.

Eudaimonia

Aristotle saw 'happiness' or *eudaimonia* as the goal in life, but argued that pleasure doesn't lead to happiness. The value of pleasure is determined by the value of the activity you are performing. If we take pleasure in good activities, the pleasure is good; if we take pleasure in bad activities, the pleasure is bad. The Good is what is good for everyone and this is *eudaimonia* — having a good quality of life and being a morally good person.

Aristotle is not talking about a state of mind, psychological happiness; he is talking about living virtuously, dealing with good and bad as best we can, while continuing to develop our virtues.

Intellectual and moral virtues

Virtues help us fulfil our function.

- Intellectual virtues are virtues of the mind such as the ability to understand, reason and make sound judgements. Intellectual virtues may be taught, like logic and mathematics.
- Moral virtues are to do with the moral character of the agent. They are not innate but are acquired through repetition and practice, like learning a musical instrument. They are 'states of character'. It is through the practice and the doing that we become a particular type of person. Aristotle argues that courage, temperance, self-discipline, generosity, friendliness, truthfulness, honesty and justice, among others, are virtues. The four cardinal virtues are prudence, temperance, fortitude and justice.

No one is virtuous by nature. You can gain moral virtues only by practice — and you are described as virtuous only once you are seen to act in a particular way, of your own free will and with honesty of intention. Pretending to be kind is not the same thing as being kind.

The doctrine of the mean

Aristotle considered it important to strike a balance — the mean or 'golden mean' — between extremes; recognising this balance leads to virtue. Developing virtues is not about being the best, but about acting in the mean between excess and deficiency. It is about choosing the right way to act with the appropriate degree of love, honesty and so on in the circumstances.

arête Innate excellence.

eudaimonia The 'good life' that Aristotle argues we are all seeking, often translated as 'happiness' or 'human flourishing'.

Exam tip

A useful point of comparison between ethical theories is their understanding of happiness and the good life.

Key quotation

The virtues are neither passions nor capacities, all that remains is that they should be states of character.

Aristotle

So, according to this, we might be angry if someone steals the car but irritated when we have misplaced the car keys. We do not want to be the person who is fearful all the time, nor the person who is not afraid enough. We want to be the person who knows when to be courageous and when to be prudent, when to feel fear and when not to.

Developing a moral character

Aristotle draws a clear distinction between passions, capacities and states of character:

- Passions refer to our bodily appetites (for food, drink and so on), our emotions, and any feelings accompanied by pleasure or pain. We don't choose our passions.
- Capacities are faculties, for example sight or mathematical ability. We have these naturally.
- Virtues are states of character: they are dispositions to act, which are freely chosen and developed out of habit.

We are born without character. Character develops over time and is shaped and moulded through practice. Aristotle suggests that it will take many years to develop a good character.

Aristotle distinguishes between voluntary and involuntary actions. Moral responsibility is about voluntary action; it involves choice. For Aristotle, choice is about deliberation — reasoned thought about how to achieve an end. The virtuous person *chooses* to act virtuously.

For Aristotle, the good life is the interaction between intellectual or practical wisdom (*phronesis*) and virtuous actions that result in a virtuous character. This produces development, which in turn produces *eudaimonia*. This is a 'virtuous circle' because virtuous acts and virtuous people are defined in terms of one another. The virtues are the only thing worth pursuing for their own sake because they will lead to *eudaimonia*.

Choosing the mean does not entail a denial of emotions. Virtue ethics allows reason to cultivate the whole person, including the emotions. It reconciles reason and emotion and overcomes the weakness of will (*akrasia*) through practical wisdom or *phronesis* based on experience and past judgements. *Phronesis* involves interpreting a moral dilemma from a holistic standpoint which acknowledges emotions and inclinations but, through pursuing the mean, allows rational choice to take precedence over irrational desires.

Temperance is a moral virtue. A temperate person abstains from indulging in bodily pleasures, is not 'self-indulgent'. A temperate person is not impassive, however. Temperance is about moderation and self-restraint, which can only be developed out of habit.

Strengths and weaknesses of virtue theory

Strengths

- The philosopher Richard Taylor (1919–2003) described virtue theory as 'an ethics of aspiration rather than an ethic of duty'. Virtue theory focuses on the growth of the moral agent — the individual rather than the act. It is not prescriptive; it doesn't tell you what to do.

Knowledge check 32

What does Aristotle mean by 'virtues'?

Key quotation

But the virtues we get by first exercising them, as also happens in the case of the arts as well. For the things we have to learn before we can do them, we learn by doing them, e.g. men become builders by building and lyreplayers by playing the lyre; so too we become just by doing just acts, temperate by doing temperate acts, brave by doing brave acts.

Aristotle

phronesis Intellectual or practical wisdom.

Knowledge check 33

What does Aristotle mean by the 'good life'?

Exam tip

A significant portion of the anthology text is about temperance. Make sure you are clear about why this is a significant virtue.

- Virtue theory offers moral guidelines which are flexible. Virtues are dispositions to act in the right way at the right time, towards the right people. Thus virtue theory adapts itself to the situation.

- For Kant, reason is all-important for following the good will; desires and inclinations lead the individual astray. Virtue ethics allows reason to develop the whole person, including the emotions.

- Virtue theory takes account of the whole person in forming a judgement about their moral worth. It does not undervalue family or community in the same way that utilitarianism and Kantian ethics do. It also recognises the paradox that life is constantly in a state of flux and change and yet we seek a consistent character. The fact that virtue theory is agent-centred makes it flexible and consistent in a way that act-centred theories are not.

- Virtue theory enables us to develop a moral education. With utilitarianism and Kantian ethics, the focus is on learning a method or principle and how to apply it, but this does not take into account the experience and constant learning that are part of life. Morality is more complex than simply 'learning the rules'. Virtue theory replaces the rules with character traits that, if developed, will help us know what the right act is nearly every time.

Weaknesses

- Critics argue that virtue ethics doesn't give us defined rules and therefore can't really help with decision-making, for example choosing between two potentially virtuous acts, particularly if I am not a virtuous person, or have not developed enough practical wisdom. Aristotle would reply that most people will have enough understanding to make moral decisions and we improve our knowledge of what is good by becoming more virtuous and practising our development of the right virtues.

- There is a problem with **moral relativism**. Virtue theory lacks universal application. Definitions of virtue will differ from community to community, and therefore decisions, too, will differ.

- Aristotle bases virtue theory on the function argument: that to live well you need to fulfil your function. Aristotle assumes we have a function, but he commits the **fallacy of composition**. If we don't have a function this undermines the idea of pursuing *eudaimonia* to fulfil our function and the theory falls apart.

- The idea of *eudaimonia* cannot be calculated and is too idealistic. How many people develop a character that causes them to act morally? How long does it take to create a 'good character', and how do we know when we have one? Do all our actions and pursuits aim at being happy and living the good life? What might make us happy might not lead to the type of moral character and good life that Aristotle envisions.

- Kant might argue that sometimes we must act out of duty and take actions that we might not see as good or ones that might not make us happy.

- There is the problem of finding the mean. First, not all actions have a mean: there is no mean to adultery, theft or murder. Acts of temperance have no mean, because temperance is itself the mean. And finding the mean is not an exact science. For example, Aristotle seems to suggest it is less of a vice to be rash than to be a coward as rashness is closer to courage than cowardice is.

Exam tip

Note down points of comparison with Kantian deontology, paying particular attention to the strengths and weaknesses of each argument. You could do this in table form.

Moral relativism The idea that ethical or moral statements do not reflect universal objective truths but make claims relative to various circumstances (social, historical, cultural and so on).

Fallacy of composition A fallacy where a conclusion about the whole is based on a truth about its part. For example, just because your eye has a function and your stomach has a function, this does not mean that you as a whole person have a function.

Modern virtue theory

Virtue theory lost momentum in the seventeenth and eighteenth centuries because it was held to be too flexible and imprecise and made it difficult to make moral decisions. However, it underwent a revival in the second half of the twentieth century because of the decline in religious values and the rejection of moral absolutes.

Alasdair MacIntyre

MacIntyre argues that virtue theory is still the best option for defining moral behaviour. He argues that our society is confused about moral behaviour, and that deontology and teleology don't really show us how to behave: they create standards that might settle key questions but, because people have different backgrounds, our moral judgements are just expressions of preference, attitude or feeling.

> **Key thinker**
>
> ### Alasdair MacIntyre (b.1929)
> MacIntyre is a Scottish philosopher who has written extensively on moral and political philosophy. His most famous work is *After Virtue* (1981).

MacIntyre argues that we live in an emotivist culture, where moral decisions depend on how we feel, and offers virtue theory as an alternative. Virtue theory, for MacIntyre, is community-based. People should aspire to be the most virtuous they can be. To this end, MacIntyre has updated Aristotle's virtues: he lists courage, justice, temperance, wisdom, industriousness, hope and patience.

MacIntyre identifies two types of good:

- internal good — a good that is specific to an activity itself and is achieved within it
- external good — something of moral value that results from the practice of a good

For example, when someone gives money to a good cause, this creates internal good as people benefit, and it creates a feeling of satisfaction for the donor. It is also an external good as it acts as a good example to others.

Philippa Foot

Foot is very critical of duty-based ethics and seeks a return to Greek ethics which advocate virtue. Some people argue that virtues may be used to a bad end, i.e. an end that isn't *eudaimonia*. Foot states that this is wrong: a virtue is only virtuous if used to the right end. Loyalty isn't a virtue if used to a bad end, for example loyalty to Hitler. The wise person directs their will to what is good and a good is something that is both intrinsically and extrinsically good. The wise or virtuous person also knows that there are particular ways of obtaining certain goods and it is these ways of obtaining goods that are the virtues.

> **Key quotation**
>
> The exercise of the virtues is itself a crucial component of the good life for man.
>
> Alasdair MacIntyre

Key thinker

Philippa Foot (1920–2010)

Foot was a British philosopher and modern virtue theorist. She created the famous trolley problem thought experiment which has since been discussed by numerous philosophers: this asks whether it would be moral to pull a lever which would prevent five people tied to a rail track from being run over by a carriage but would kill one person tied to a second track.

Foot also characterises virtues as 'correctives'. She likens humans to planks of wood that are left out to season. Wood naturally warps and changes shape and it needs continual attention to make it straight. Virtues do the same for the human character: they continually straighten us out so that eventually we can, through habit, become virtuous.

Key quotation

Anyone who thinks about it can see that for human beings the teaching and following of morality is something necessary.

Philippa Foot

Is virtue theory compatible with religious approaches to ethics?

Virtue theory has a long history of being applied and adapted to fit the purpose of Christian ethics. Aquinas drew inspiration from Aristotle in his understanding of the universe and its purpose and in his view that there are four cardinal virtues. Virtue theory is compatible with a religious way of life, with a focus on flourishing and happiness achieved through the development of a moral character.

However, philosophers like Foot argue that religious approaches to ethics and virtue ethics are not really compatible because religious doctrines on morality are fundamentally legalistic and inflexible, and virtue theory isn't. Richard Taylor goes further and argues that virtue theory and religious ethics have completely opposite purposes: Christianity argues that the meek should inherit the earth, so Christians are not encouraged to develop their moral character and to become better and greater. Christianity, in Taylor's view, encourages mediocrity and weakness.

However, we could be critical of this view. Christianity encourages moral development and sees Jesus as an example of this. Virtue theory asks us to aspire to be virtuous, and we can achieve that through taking the example of virtuous people as role models and adopting their virtues. Thus, it could be argued that virtue theory and a religious approach to ethics can complement one another.

Knowledge check 34

According to Aristotle, how do we fulfil our function?

Comparison of Kant and Aristotle: summary

- Kant's ethical theory is deontological — it emphasises the intention in performing an action rather than the consequence. It is absolute and universal.
- Kant believed that we can discover ethical action through reason — we don't need to rely on God. The only thing that matters is having the good will.
- Hypothetical imperatives are commands that are true only in certain situations so cannot form the basis of a moral system. Categorical imperatives simply say 'Do this' and are not dependent on the person or the situation.
- The categorical imperative has three formulations, the first two of which are universalisability and the requirement not to treat others solely as an end.
- Kant gives us clear guidelines and rules for acting morally, but these guidelines do not provide us with flexibility, for example where there are conflicting duties or in cases where there is a motivation other than duty (e.g. commitment to family).
- W. D. Ross argues that moral decisions should be based on *prima facie* duties, duties which are binding and can be overridden only if they clash with other duties.
- Thomas Nagel argues that moral decision-making should be based on agent-relative rather than agent-neutral reasons. Deontology is part of agent-centred ethics.
- Virtue ethics is about the development of character. It seeks to find a less rigid way of deciding our moral duty and how we should behave.
- Virtue theory argues that the function of humans is to reason and using reason allows us to develop a virtuous character, which in turns means we can attain the good life — *eudaimonia*.
- Aristotle argues that the idea of the mean, or choosing to behave in a way that is not extreme, should lead us to a good life.
- The attraction of virtue theory is mainly in its practical nature. It is a way of living and a lifelong journey, and can be learnt through example and practice.
- The problem with virtue theory is that while it might create a 'good character', it does not give us guidelines on how to act in any particular situation and therefore the decision on how to act remains subjective.
- Virtue ethics has been revived by modern philosophers such as Philippa Foot and Alasdair MacIntyre.

■ Medical ethics: beginning and end of life issues

Issues in medical ethics with a focus on beginning and end of life debates

We know when life begins, but when does the right to life begin? Similarly, is there any circumstance where it is justifiable to end someone's life, with or without their consent? The argument at the heart of such matters is the issue of personhood.

Personhood

See also the Key thinker box on Peter Singer in the section on environmental issues (p. 16).

When we refer to a 'human being' we are referring to a member of the species *Homo sapiens*, but when we refer to a 'person' we are referring to someone with particular characteristics such as personality, self-awareness, the ability to use language, a network of beliefs, a consciousness of its own experiences, rationality and so on. Joseph Fletcher, for example, identified the indicators of personhood as self-awareness, self-control, a sense of the future, a sense of the past, a capacity to relate to others, concern for others, communication and curiosity.

Personhood is central to many medical ethical debates because, in our society, it is generally considered to be morally wrong to kill a person but not morally wrong to kill a non-person. This is not as straightforward as it sounds. It seems sensible to argue that a dead body is an 'ex-person'. But what about someone with brainstem death who has no possibility of regaining consciousness, or a person with severe dementia? In these cases, the personality we once knew is no longer present; they are diminished persons. Likewise, if we feel that a foetus is no more than a potential person, we may feel that abortion is allowable; if not, we may question its morality.

Sanctity of life vs quality of life

Modern liberal societies increasingly focus on quality of life over the traditional, often religious **sanctity of life argument**. Singer rejects sanctity of life arguments as absolutist and dependent on an outdated Christian view of ethics. While the sanctity of life argument states that human life is sacred, making any form of killing wrong, **quality of life arguments** seek to show that, in certain circumstances, it is better to end a life.

Singer also rejects the idea that humans are a 'special' form of life. In *Practical Ethics*, he defines the idea of sanctity 'to be no more than a way of saying that human life has some special value, a value quite distinct from the value of the lives of other living things'.

Both arguments are now facing problems in the light of medical advances. People are now able to live longer and overcome disabilities and illnesses that would have previously caused death. But should we, or do we want to, preserve that life?

> **Key quotation**
>
> The notion that human life is sacred just because it is human life is medieval.
>
> Peter Singer

Sanctity of life argument
The argument that life is sacred and has a God-given purpose.

Quality of life argument
The idea that the overall wellbeing of a person is a significant factor in making medical or life-or-death decisions.

Jonathan Glover on bioethics

In *Causing Death and Saving Lives* (1977), Glover argues that a universal moral system is impossible to achieve. While most of us agree that torture and killing are wrong, and the sanctity of life argument is still widely upheld, we make exceptions when it comes to turning off life-support machines, or the abortion of disabled foetuses.

> **Key thinker**
>
> ### Jonathan Glover (b.1941)
> Glover is a British philosopher and professor emeritus at King's College London with a specialism in bioethics. He was the chair of a European Commission Working Party on Assisted Reproduction and won the Dan David Prize for outstanding contribution to bioethics, culture and science in 2018.

Glover argues that a pro-life defence in the case of abortion and euthanasia is untenable. Modern science can keep alive human beings who would normally have died, but in some instances their quality of life is poor and their suffering is unjustifiable. Glover accepts that broad legislation on euthanasia, especially, is difficult because not all cases are the same. He stresses the importance of frank discussions between doctors and patients, and careful assessment of each case.

Beginning of life: the status of the embryo

The human embryo develops in stages:

- conception to 14 days: pre-embryo
- 14 days to 8 weeks: embryo
- 8 weeks onwards: foetus

We know when biological life begins — with fertilisation and the unique mixing of two sets of DNA — but at what stage does the embryo or foetus become an actual person with rights? Does it happen at conception, at implantation, when brain activity begins, when the foetus becomes viable or at the moment of birth?

To know how to act, we need a much more definite idea of when life begins. We need to consider religious and sociobiological factors too. For example:

- Dualism is the argument that a person is made up of a body and a soul/mind, which is separate. Religious believers maintain the soul is implanted by God and, for many, ensoulment takes place from conception.
- The relational aspect of personhood means that a human being becomes a person when accepted as such by others. Personhood then becomes a matter of social convention.

Embryo research

An embryo contains stem cells, the building blocks of all the tissues and organs of a human being. In the laboratory, embryonic stem cells are derived from the blastula, an early embryo of less than 100 cells, which cannot survive very long unless implanted into a woman's womb.

Knowledge check 35

Why is the question of personhood important in medical ethics?

In the UK, the law states that research, experimentation and testing on embryos can only take place up to 14 days after fertilisation. After that time, it is argued, an individual person starts to develop.

Some would argue that destroying a blastula in order to harvest its cells is essentially destroying an unborn child. In this view, the embryo has moral status from the point of fertilisation; it is a potential person.

On the other hand, an embryo has none of the psychological, emotional or physical properties we associate with personhood and, unless implanted into a womb, the blastula has no chance of survival and growth.

Why do we need to create embryos?

- Embryonic stem cell research is a valuable tool in the search for cures for genetic illnesses and other long-term medical conditions such as Parkinson's or Alzheimer's diseases.
- Couples who have fertility problems may be helped to conceive using *in vitro* fertilisation (IVF), where an embryo is grown in the laboratory and subsequently implanted into the mother's uterus. In most cases, more embryos than necessary are created and only those that show the best potential for successful implantation are implanted. Controversially, the rest may be destroyed after a certain period of time.
- Pre-implantation genetic diagnosis or PGD involves creating an embryo in a lab, removing a single cell after five days and carrying out genetic testing on it. Doctors are able to check for genetic conditions known to be present in the family, or considered possible, such as Down's syndrome or cystic fibrosis. They can also determine the sex of the embryo (which may be of relevance to particular conditions) or even determine whether the child might eventually be able to help treat a sick sibling. Armed with this information, the couple decide whether to implant the embryo.

Why do we need to use embryo stem cells?

Cord blood is the blood that remains in the placenta and umbilical cord after a baby is born and this too is rich in stem cells. However, cord blood stem cells are classified as adult stem cells. Adult stem cells can only differentiate into a limited number of cell types so embryonic stem cells have much greater potential for the treatment of disease or injury.

Religious views on embryo research

Natural law theory, and thus Catholic thinking, wholly rejects embryonic stem cell research, first because it involves procreation outside of marriage and a loving sexual relationship, but also because human beings ought to be created in the womb. An attempt to create human beings in any other way is a failure to worship God and undermines the stability of society.

In the Catholic tradition, donation of organs and tissue — including the placenta, umbilical cord or cord blood — is encouraged. So, too, is the therapeutic use of stem cells, so long as their use does not involve the destruction of embryonic human life. The decision to donate lies with the parents.

Key quotation

Human life is sacred and inviolable and the use of prenatal diagnosis for selective purposes should be discouraged with strength.

Pope Francis, 2019

Content Guidance

The most significant issue for Catholics in current debates about the donation and banking of umbilical cord blood is to work out how this new resource should be made available. Should a couple be encouraged to store their child's umbilical cord blood for possible future use by themselves, their own children or members of their own family? Or should it be donated to a cord blood bank and used for people who need it because they are sick?

Abortion

The arguments for and against abortion have been presented time and time again, and yet there is still no consensus.

In Great Britain (but not in Northern Ireland), the situation is as follows:

- The law requires that two doctors give their consent before a pregnancy is terminated.
- An abortion can take place up to 24 weeks after conception.
- An abortion can be performed after this period if there is a risk that the mother will be permanently injured by continuing with the pregnancy, or if the child is found to have a serious disability.

Doctors take psychological and social factors into account as well as medical factors.

The religious viewpoint

Natural law and the Catholic Church argue that the natural consequence of a woman becoming pregnant is to give birth. Other religious groups accept that there are certain situations in which abortion might be permissible, for example after rape.

Overall, religious views are against abortion:

- Only God has the right to decide when a person should die.
- Each person has an eternal soul and this should be protected.
- Life is God-given. Once life is devalued by legally and morally destroying life, then all life is under threat.

In Islam, abortion is considered wrong, but is not a punishable wrong if it is performed in the first 120 days of pregnancy, if the mother's life is at risk or if the foetus is not viable.

The freedom or pro-choice argument

'Pro-choice' is not 'pro-abortion'. The argument is about who should decide. Those who support a pro-choice position argue that a woman should be free to decide whether or not to have an abortion:

- The foetus is part of a woman's body until it is capable of independent life. The woman has the right to decide because at that stage life is potential not actual.
- Giving birth must be seen within the overall situation in which a woman finds herself in terms of personal development and social, family or financial circumstances.

The issue of personhood is again key. The two central issues are:

- whether the foetus is a person or a potential person
- whether the foetus has rights and, if so, how to balance these against the rights of the mother

Knowledge check 36

Why does the Roman Catholic Church consider embryonic stem cell research and PGD to be immoral?

Key quotation

Is it permissible to contract a hitman to solve a problem?
Pope Francis, 2018

A defence of abortion: Judith Jarvis Thomson

In her 1971 paper 'A Defence of Abortion', Judith Jarvis Thomson used an imaginative thought experiment to explore the idea of abortion:

> You wake up in the morning and find yourself back to back in bed with an unconscious violinist. A famous unconscious violinist. He has been found to have a fatal kidney ailment, and the Society of Music Lovers has canvassed all the available medical records and found that you alone have the right blood type to help. They have therefore kidnapped you, and last night the violinist's circulatory system was plugged into yours, so that your kidneys can be used to extract poisons from his blood as well as your own. [If he is unplugged from you now, he will die; but] in nine months he will have recovered from his ailment, and can safely be unplugged from you.

Thomson argues that you are entitled to unplug yourself from the violinist because the right to life does not entail the right to use another person's body. Likewise, abortion does not violate the foetus's right to life but merely deprives the foetus of something — the use of the pregnant woman's body — to which it has no right.

This argument only really seems to work in cases of abortion after rape and there are a number of objections:

- If the pregnant woman has voluntarily engaged in sex, she is responsible for the foetus's need to use her body; she has no such responsibility towards the violinist.
- The pregnant woman has a special obligation to sustain her offspring; the violinist confers no such obligation.
- There is a moral difference between killing and allowing to die.

The American philosopher Don Marquis (b.1935) argues that abortion is wrong, not because of the personhood of the foetus but because abortion deprives the foetus of a 'future like ours'. The main strength of this argument is that it removes the problem of whether the foetus is a person with rights. If it is wrong to kill a child or adult on the ground that they are being deprived of a future, the same argument applies to a foetus.

Although this argument seems viable, it would seem to suggest that abortion is not wrong in cases where the foetus is disabled to the extent that it would not be capable of having any meaningful future experiences — or if its experiences would be unpleasant or painful.

The end of life: euthanasia

Euthanasia means allowing doctors to end the lives of their patients. It is illegal in the UK for a doctor actively to kill their patient, but they may take the decision to facilitate a patient's death by some other means, for example by withdrawing life-preserving treatment or food.

Assisted dying means something slightly different: here, the dying person controls their own death with the assistance of a third party. This is also illegal in the UK.

Exam tip

In your exam answers, make clear distinctions between different types of euthanasia.

Content Guidance

Voluntary euthanasia

Voluntary euthanasia is carried out at the request of the person dying, for example if life has become unbearable and they have no hope of recovery.

One argument against voluntary euthanasia is that while people are in a great deal of pain, depressed, or perhaps being medicated to relieve their symptoms, they may not be thinking clearly enough to make a valid choice.

Opponents of voluntary euthanasia argue that it may lead to a slippery slope of people feeling pressurised into agreeing to euthanasia, perhaps in the belief that family members can't or don't want to look after them.

Non-voluntary euthanasia

Non-voluntary euthanasia involves individuals who are not capable of understanding the choice between life and death, for example a person with severe Down's syndrome, a young child or someone in the later stages of dementia. Here the choice is being made for them, 'in their best interests'.

Opponents of non-voluntary euthanasia also argue from a slippery slope perspective. A person may not be able to express a choice about life and death, but this does not mean they do not have quality of life. Even if the patient has left a request for euthanasia, we cannot rule out the possibility of future treatments.

Good or bad medical practice?

Michael Wilcockson considers euthanasia from a medical ethics perspective and explains why it is still illegal in the UK.

The British Medical Association (BMA) argues that there is a difference between actively ending someone's life and allowing a patient to die with dignity. The BMA is against **active euthanasia** but accepts **passive euthanasia**.

Moral crisis in liberal societies

Wilcockson refers to Singer's argument that modern liberal societies focus more on quality of life than sanctity of life. Doctors face increasingly difficult decisions, as illustrated by two very different cases:

- Tony Nicklinson, who had locked-in syndrome after suffering a stroke in 2005, was denied the right to have treatment, food and water withdrawn. Medical institutions argued he still had quality of life, something he denied. He died at 58, six days after losing his court case.
- In 2017, the parents of baby Charlie Gard, who had a rare, life-limiting genetic condition, challenged the decision of the medical professionals at Great Ormond Street Hospital (GOSH) that it was in Charlie's best interest to withdraw mechanical ventilation and to allow him to die. The High Court ruled in favour of GOSH and the European Court of Human Rights refused to intervene. Charlie was transferred to a hospice and died the day after mechanical ventilation was withdrawn, at 11 months 24 days of age.

Three moral principles

Wilcockson argues that the three moral principles used by doctors arise out of the Hippocratic Oath and draw on the distinction between active and passive euthanasia.

Exam tip

Michael Wilcockson's article 'Euthanasia and Doctors' Ethics' (1999) is an anthology text.

Use this link to access the *Anthology*: https://tinyurl.com/yargzcu6

Section B of Paper 2 will consist of a two-part question on an excerpt from an anthology text.

Active euthanasia An action taken to end a life, for example a lethal injection.

Passive euthanasia Allowing someone to die by withholding treatment or food.

Key quotation

The moral basis for sustaining life and allowing death is in transition.

Michael Wilcockson

These principles concern acts and omissions, double effect, and ordinary and extraordinary means, as discussed below.

Acts and omissions

An act is performed by an agent who actively intervenes to bring about a foreseeable outcome. Active euthanasia is an act.

An omission is a failure to act but with an awareness of what the result of not acting will be. Passive euthanasia is an omission.

Wilcockson argues that failure to act does not absolve you from moral responsibility. If a pacifist refuses to shoot someone, for example, their failure to act is an active moral decision. The Catholic Church takes a clear stance on this: there is no distinction between act and omission — or between active and passive euthanasia — if the intention is to relieve suffering and the known outcome is death. By this argument, withholding treatment from Charlie Gard was closer to active than passive euthanasia.

The doctrine of double effect

The doctrine of double effect draws a distinction between foreseeing an outcome (death) and choosing to act specifically to bring about that outcome. Thus, administering potentially lethal doses of pain-killing drugs to relieve suffering is moral, and in the UK legal, provided the person giving the drugs does not primarily intend to kill the patient.

Wilcockson is critical of this doctrine on the grounds that it could easily be open to abuse and that there is no real distinction between intending to act and foreseeing the consequences of an action.

Ordinary and extraordinary means

Ordinary versus extraordinary means is a distinction used by both quality of life and sanctity of life arguments. The Catholic position is to allow people to die as God would have them die. In most circumstances we have a duty to accept healthcare (ordinary means), but we do not have to go to extremes and keep ourselves going when this is simply prolonging the dying process or is associated with grave suffering (extraordinary means). Treatment is considered 'extraordinary' if it has been determined that it is not going to work to keep the person alive or to reverse the course of the disease, or if the burdens of that treatment are disproportionate to the benefits.

Natural law arguments used by the Catholic Church state that a person who refuses food and water, which are life-sustaining, is committing suicide. However, refusing life-prolonging treatment is not suicide, if there is no chance of recovery. This is the weak sanctity of life argument. Providing food, water and palliative care is an ordinary means, while a life-prolonging treatment that strips a person of their dignity can be considered extraordinary means. Withdrawal of this treatment is letting nature take its course.

The BMA approves of this as long as the patient is mentally able to make that decision. However, if a doctor feels that treatment should be pursued but stops it because it is against the patient's wishes, it could be considered assisted dying.

> **Key quotation**
>
> A person may cause evil to others not only by his actions but by his inaction, and in either case he is justly accountable to them for the injury.
>
> J. S. Mill

Palliative care
Measures to make a terminally ill patient comfortable and alleviate pain and other symptoms.

Proportionate and disproportionate means

Wilcockson argues that it may be better to refer to proportionate and disproportionate means, a distinction also used by the natural law tradition. This allows doctors to decide on a case-by-case basis what is in the best interest of the patient.

■ Proportionate means is any treatment that, in the given circumstances, offers a reasonable hope of benefit to the patient, judged holistically within the context of the whole person, their physical and mental health and their personal, financial, familial and social circumstances. Generally, a treatment or means is not too burdensome when it offers benefits that outweigh the burdens to the patient and others.

■ A disproportionate means is any treatment that, in the given circumstances, either offers no reasonable hope of benefit or carries burdens or risks disproportionate to its expected benefits.

This distinction becomes difficult with 'non-competent patients', for example a severely ill baby who has no chance of recovery. The weak sanctity of life argument would argue that a doctor must act with care and compassion and make the baby as comfortable as possible, while not prolonging treatment for a baby who has no chance of survival. The quality of life argument relies on utilitarian arguments and considers a variety of factors, weighing the side effects of medication against the benefits to the patient. However, it is hard to set clear criteria: doctors need to consider available resources as well as what makes someone's life valuable.

Law and morality

The liberal view of ethics is based on Mill's harm principle. Thus suicide is no longer illegal, but it remains illegal to help someone commit suicide. The liberal principle of personal autonomy means that I have the right to make my own decisions about how I lead my life; in the context of medical ethics, this means the right to refuse or choose my treatment. This has implications for how we understand the connection between law and morality.

The law refers to rules prescribed by the state in order to protect society. Citizens have a duty to obey these laws. Morality, on the other hand, deals with issues of right and wrong and shared values in society. Liberals draw a distinction between the private and public spheres. Law is a public matter, morality is private. Law should thus be divorced from morality. The function of the law stays within the harm principle. If the law becomes a moral guideline it leads to what Mill calls the 'tyranny of the majority'.

However, Wilcockson argues that in practice this may not be possible. Although law is detached from morality, it takes into account a general moral feeling and legislation is decided on the basis of how society morally feels. The moral feeling among doctors, if we base it on the BMA's argument, is that doctors do not want euthanasia to be legalised because it could lead to a slippery slope and allow for other forms of killing. It also goes against the role of doctors, which is to save patients.

Wilcockson identifies two main arguments against legalising euthanasia. These concern the 'thin end of the wedge' and the undermining of autonomy, as discussed below.

Knowledge check 37

In relation to euthanasia debates, what are proportionate and disproportionate means?

Key quotation

In practice, though, the law has to take into account a general moral feeling and it has also to acknowledge that once legislation takes place, in the mind of many this is seen to give tacit approval to certain forms of behaviour.

Michael Wilcockson

The wedge argument

The slippery slope or 'thin end of the wedge' argument refers to the concern that legalised euthanasia would lead to other forms of killing becoming accepted and legal: if voluntary euthanasia becomes legal, involuntary euthanasia could become legal too.

Critics such as Peter Singer have argued that there is no empirical evidence for a wedge effect, for example from the Netherlands where euthanasia is legal under strictly controlled conditions.

Undermining personal autonomy

The BMA has voiced concerns that legalising euthanasia in order to respect individual autonomy actually undermines it, especially if the individual is vulnerable. The trust between doctor and patient would be broken, and society's attitudes towards disability, age and illness would change.

Exam tip

In evaluative essays which require synoptic links, make connections between ethical theories, the study of religion and euthanasia. Reference to natural moral law in the context of euthanasia is a good example of a synoptic link.

Issues in medical ethics: summary

- Ethical debates surrounding the beginning of life are concerned with the status of the embryo and whether/when it has rights as a person.
- Religious views tend to focus on the sanctity of life and argue that an embryo is a potential person from the time of conception, and that destroying it is killing.
- Secular approaches focus on quality of life and what is in the best interest of the individual and the family.
- Religious and secular views inform attitudes to medical advances like embryo stem cell research and pre-implantation genetic diagnosis.
- There are different types of euthanasia; the most important of these from a medical ethics perspective are voluntary and non-voluntary euthanasia.
- As with abortion, the issue of euthanasia rests on ideas of personhood and on sanctity of life and quality of life arguments.
- The British Medical Association is against the legalisation of euthanasia on the grounds that it goes against the Hippocratic Oath and undermines the role of the doctor as someone who tries to save lives.
- Religious views on euthanasia tend to argue against it, although some make a distinction between proportionate and disproportionate means to preserve life and consider whether there is any benefit to treatment for someone with a terminal illness.
- Liberal principles on euthanasia argue that euthanasia is a private matter and that individuals should be free to choose what is in their best interest.

Questions & Answers

How to use this section

In this section, you will be introduced to the types of questions you will need to answer in your AS and A-level examinations. The AS and A-level papers utilise the same **command words** — Explore, Assess and Analyse for both AS and A-level papers; Clarify and Evaluate for the A-level examination only. There are five sample questions in this section, each demonstrating one of the five command words.

The sample questions are all representative of the A-level examination and may cover topics not included in the AS specification. However, exam tips and examiner commentary provide information of specific relevance for students preparing for the AS examination. In line with the format of the A-level papers, the questions are numbered 1, 2, 3a, 3b and 4.

Immediately below each question is a commentary to help you recognise and understand what you are required to do. The commentary is indicated by the icon **e**.

For each sample question, there are two sample student answers. Answer A is a lower-level answer and answer B is a higher-level answer.

Below each sample answer, you will see an analysis of what to look out for when answering each question type, the mark awarded, and the examiner's comments, indicated by the icon **e**. The examiner's comments will highlight the strengths and weaknesses of the answer to identify areas for improvement, specific problems and common errors such as lack of clarity, weak or non-existent development, irrelevance and misinterpretation of the question or key terms.

There is a 'levels'-based approach to marking the questions that comprise both the AS and A-level Paper 2. This means the examiner makes an initial assessment of the quality of the answer and places it in a level ranging from 1 to 5, depending on the question, and then refines their judgement to award a more precise mark within that level. This enables freedom in how you respond but you must still satisfy the requirements as indicated by the command word used.

> **Exam tip**
>
> It is recommended that you refer to the levels descriptors provided in the sample assessment materials for Religious Studies produced by Pearson Edexcel. The AS sample assessment materials are available at: https://tinyurl.com/y6w9k9bc (pages 13–18). The A-level sample assessment materials are available at: https://tinyurl.com/yd2tgjdr (pages 19–25).

Command word A key word that indicates how you should answer a question. For example, 'Clarify' suggests you should identify key ideas and explain key concepts.

> **Exam tip**
>
> Remember, for your AS examination, you will need to answer questions which require you to *explore, assess* and *analyse*. For your A-level examination, you must answer questions which require you to *explore, assess, clarify, analyse* and *evaluate*. Refer to Appendix 1 of the specification for further guidance on what each command word means — available at: https://tinyurl.com/ybxf6gg3 (page 79).

Exam format

AS

The AS Religious Studies Paper 2, Religion and Ethics, is a written examination which will account for 33.3% of your AS Religious Studies qualification. You will have *1 hour* to complete the paper, which is worth *54 marks*. The paper comprises *two* sections and you will answer *all* the questions in Section A and Section B.

- In **Section A** there will be three extended, open-response questions:
  - Question 1 will use the command word 'Explore' and is worth 8 marks.
  - Questions 2 and 3 will use the command word 'Assess' and are each worth 9 marks.
- In **Section B**, there will be one two-part essay question related to a theme:
  - Question 4a will use the command word 'Explore' and is worth 8 marks.
  - Question 4b will use the command word 'Analyse' and is worth 20 marks.

A-level

The A-level Religious Studies Paper 2, Religion and Ethics, is a written exam paper, also accounting for 33.3% of your A-level qualification. You have *2 hours* to complete the paper, which is worth *80 marks*. The paper comprises *three* sections and you will answer *all* the questions in Sections A, B and C.

- In **Section A** there will be two questions:
  - Question 1 will use the command word 'Explore' and is worth 8 marks.
  - Question 2 will use the command word 'Assess' and is worth 12 marks.
- In **Section B** there will be one question, question 3, divided into two parts (a and b). You must answer both parts. There will be an extract from the 'Religion and Ethics' section of the *A Level Religious Studies Anthology* that you will be asked to clarify and assess.
  - Question 3a will use the command word 'Clarify' and will ask for a clarification of the ideas presented in the extract. This part of the question is worth 10 marks.
  - Question 3b will use the command word 'Analyse'. This part of the question is worth 20 marks.
- In **Section C** there will be one question. In your answer you will be required to discuss how the ideas from Religion and Ethics have been influenced by either Study of Religion (for example Christianity) or Philosophy of Religion.
  - Question 4 will use the command word 'Evaluate' and is worth 30 marks.

> **Exam tip**
>
> You are expected to study a range of texts across any suitable topic area. These are published in the *A Level Religious Studies Anthology*, Paper 2, Religion and Ethics, which can be downloaded from the Pearson Edexcel website or from this link: https://tinyurl.com/yargzcu6.

■ Question 1: Explore

Question 1

Explore the work of one leading figure in the fight for equality. (8 marks)

(e) The command word 'Explore' requires you to demonstrate understanding by investigating different reasons, concepts and ideas.

In this question you are being asked to show knowledge and understanding of the views of one leading figure in the fight for equality. You need to choose one from gender, race or disability equality. For example, Martin Luther King is a key figure for race equality and Joni Eareckson Tada is a key figure for disability. You first need to be clear why there is an issue with gender, race or disability equality, and then describe how your chosen figure has helped progress to be made in the fight for equality.

For the AS paper, you should aim to spend 8 minutes. For the A-level paper, you should spend around 10 minutes. You will not have time to write about all the views expressed by your chosen thinker but, in order to achieve level 3, you must show knowledge and understanding of a range of ideas.

> **Exam tip**
>
> 'Explore' is both an AS and A-level command word, with questions always worth 8 marks. On the AS exam paper, questions 1 and 4a will use the command word 'Explore'. On the A-level paper it will be question 1 only. This sample question is taken from the A-level only part of the specification.

> **Student answer A**
>
> Martin Luther King advocated affirmative non-violent actions that entailed marches, silent protests and sit-ins to combat racism and segregation in America in the twentieth century. King considered how black people were constantly being discriminated against, leaving many of them unemployed. His famous 'I have a dream' speech, where he argued that he was hopeful for a nation where there would be no more discrimination against black people and where black children would be able to access a good education and good job opportunities, led him to be assassinated. King started off with a small amount of people but soon there were hundreds of people fighting against racism. a Many critics argue that his protests were provocative and a threat to the protesters' lives because, while they were not violent, the response from the authorities could be. b

(e) **Level 1 awarded.**

a The focus on Martin Luther King is good but the response is too narrow and general. It needs to develop the context and explain more clearly why there was an issue with inequality, as well as justifying how and why King tried to address it. It also needs development on the Christian element of his thought. b The last statement is evaluative and doesn't meet the specific demands of the question.

Student answer B

A prominent figure in the fight for race equality was Martin Luther King. King was a Christian preacher who fought to end racism and segregation in 1960s' America. At the time, black people did not enjoy the same rights as white people when it came to education, employment, healthcare and access to facilities such as shops or transport. **a** Martin Luther King instigated silent protests and marches which initially started after a black woman, Rosa Parks, refused to sit at the back of a bus as segregation laws demanded. King's belief that segregation had to end stemmed from his Christian conviction that all are born equal. He felt however that pacifism was the key to ending inequality and was inspired by Jesus's commitment to non-violence: this is because love is at the core of the Christian faith and King felt that making society fairer should not be achieved through violent action. **b** King's actions were an integral part of the civil rights movement which led to the end of unjust policies of segregation and a greater commitment to equality. **c**

e Level 3 awarded.

a This answer explains the background to Martin Luther King's actions: the segregation experienced by black people, why a fight for equality was necessary and **b** the fact that King's Christian faith lay at the core of his politics of non-violence. **c** Ideas are well developed and integrated and the answer is comprehensive enough for an 8-mark question.

■ Question 2: Assess

Question 2

Assess the weaknesses of act and rule utilitarianism.

(12 marks)

e The command word 'Assess' is asking you to demonstrate knowledge and understanding of the issue raised in the question *and* to provide 'reasoned argument of factors to reach a judgement regarding their importance/relevance to the question context'.

The question requires you to focus on the weaknesses of utilitarianism, but because of the command word 'Assess', you need to explain whether those weaknesses could be overcome. For example, if you said that a weakness of act utilitarianism is that it could justify immoral actions, you could assess it by saying that rule utilitarianism and ideal utilitarianism attempt to solve this issue.

In 'Assess' questions you will be awarded fewer marks for AO1, knowledge and understanding, and more marks for AO2, the quality of the arguments you put forward. At A-level, as in this sample question, with 12 marks available, this means 4 marks for AO1 and 8 marks for AO2. At AS, where the 'Assess' questions are worth 9 marks, this means 3 marks for AO1 and 6 marks for AO2.

You should aim to spend 10 minutes on this question on the AS paper, and 20 minutes on this question on the A-level paper.

Exam tip

'Assess' is both an AS and A-level command word. On the AS exam paper, questions 2 and 3 will use the command word 'Assess'. On the A-level paper it will be question 2 only. This sample question is taken from the A-level only part of the specification and is worth 12 marks. At AS level 'Assess' questions are worth 9 marks.

Student answer A

A key strength of utilitarianism is its secular nature; the rules are separate from divine command theory and therefore can easily be applied to everyday life. However, utilitarianism can be criticised for the fact that it is too simplistic. Human beings value other things besides hedonism, such as moral integrity. **a**

A second strength is that utilitarianism is universal: it transcends cultural barriers because its starting point is human nature. However, it does not take into account that two acts may result in the same amount of pleasure, but one might involve something else immoral. Utilitarianism can appear to justify actions which are generally held to be morally inexcusable. **b** For example, three prison guards may get an amount of pleasure out of torturing a prisoner that outweighs the prisoner's pain, but most people would argue that torture is immoral and unjust. Moreover, utilitarianism doesn't take into account personal responsibilities. For example, when faced with the prospect of only being able to save your elderly father or a doctor with the power to save many lives, utilitarian thinking would argue you must save the doctor because he or she could bring the greatest happiness. However, most people would put their loved ones first.

Rule utilitarianism tries to solve some of these problems, but many other significant issues arise. **c** For example, what happens if someone wants to break the rule because this would have more utility than obeying it, for example killing in self-defence? If there are exceptions to the rules then is there really a rule at all? Also, the distinction between higher and lower pleasures is hard to define and if there are disputes over what is a 'higher' pleasure, this may cause class/wealth divides and inevitably would not lead to the greatest happiness for the greatest number. **d**

e Level 2 awarded.

a The AO1 content which requires analysis of both theories is quite implicit. This answer shows some understanding of some of the key weaknesses of act and rule utilitarianism but it lacks precision. **b** For example, the second paragraph does not make it clear that the student is talking about act utilitarianism — the view that we should consider the morality of an action on a case-by-case basis, as opposed to rule utilitarianism. The weaknesses are not assessed very clearly. **c** For example, the third paragraph states that rule utilitarianism solves the issues with act utilitarianism but doesn't specify why. **d** Finally, it lacks a clear conclusion which offers a point of view on the question. The 12-mark questions require students to construct coherent and reasoned judgements of the full range of elements in the question: while a range of knowledge is present in this response, a clear judgement is not present.

Student answer B

Utilitarianism is an ethical theory which argues that what is good is based on its consequences; the motive is irrelevant. Hedonistic utilitarianism argues that an action is moral if it brings pleasure to the majority. This means that the amount of pleasure should outweigh any pain involved. Jeremy Bentham created the hedonic calculus to help determine which action produces the greatest pleasure or utility. This considers factors like how many people are involved, the duration of the pain/pleasure and how much pain/pleasure is created. At first glance this theory sounds solid; however, there are many weaknesses that could undermine the entire theory.

Act utilitarianism bases morality purely on actions and consequences and says we should judge each situation on its merits as we come to it. While this gives us flexibility, we can't always accurately weigh up the consequences of an action and it could justify immoral actions. For example, if ten people gain pleasure from one person's suffering, does their pleasure outweigh the victim's pain? Following act utilitarianism, most likely we would decide that the sacrifice of one person brings the biggest pleasure for the group, therefore it is a moral action, but that goes against our moral intuitions.

Rule utilitarianism attempts to resolve this issue by saying that we should focus on moral rules which bring maximum utility. Thus, there would be a moral rule not to kill. However, it is unclear whether we should follow the rule because it is the rule or because it has good consequences. For example, if there is a rule not to kill but I need to kill one hostage to save the other 19 hostages (as otherwise all the hostages will die), it seems that the most moral thing to do is to kill the one, as this is what has the most utility. [a]

Rule utilitarianism also makes a distinction between higher and lower pleasures; for example, sex would be considered a lower pleasure and reading a higher pleasure. This helps rule utilitarians to avoid condoning immoral acts. This can be demonstrated if we look at the group of ten harming the single victim. The pleasure that the ten people get is a lower pleasure and therefore would not outweigh the pain of the single victim. The problem with this is that it can be difficult to define which pleasures are higher or lower, and to know the difference we need to have experienced both. [b]

Rule utilitarianism helps us to stick to a set code that a whole society could follow. This is useful for younger people who don't have much life experience as it gives them an example to follow and they don't necessarily need to assess each situation individually. This makes rule utilitarianism more practical. However, if we have a rule saying you can never lie, and a murderer comes and asks you where your friend is, logically you have to tell them and this could put your friend in extreme danger. Having absolute rules can make rules difficult to follow and can at times cause more pain and suffering than being a little more flexible.

Both types of utilitarianism only account for the majority of people and could allow for a minority to suffer. Many people would see this as immoral and undermining the arguments of both act and rule utilitarianism. There are many strengths and weaknesses of both arguments but overall there are more negatives to these theories than there are positives. **c**

e Level 3 awarded.

This answer is effective in showing knowledge and understanding of the two theories, that is, both act and rule utilitarianism. **a** The analysis of both theories is thorough and the structure of the answer is clear so that there is a coherent and logical chain of reasoning. Each paragraph identifies a key weakness but also explains how it could be overcome. **b** A range of evaluative points is given and there are clear examples given to develop the reasoning. **c** There is a clear judgement at the end which answers the question; this is essential to getting into the top band.

■ Question 3a: Clarify (A-level only)

Question 3a

Clarify the ideas illustrated in this passage about situation ethics' understanding of love.

You must refer to the passage in your response.

(10 marks)

> ### Extract: William Barclay on situation ethics
>
> The situationist is not talking about what we might call romantic love. In Greek there are four words for love, there is *erōs*, which means passion; there is always sex in *erōs*. There is *philia*, which is friendship-feeling; there is physical love in *philia*, but there is loyalty and companionship as well. There is *storgē*, which is love in the family circle; there is no sex in it; it is the love of a father for a daughter, a son for his mother, a brother for a sister. And there is *agapē*; this is the word. *Agapē* is unconquerable goodwill; it is the determination always to seek the other man's highest good, no matter what he does to you. Insult, injury, indifference — it does not matter; nothing but goodwill. It has been defined as purpose, not passion. It is an attitude to the other person.
>
> This is all important, because if we talk about this kind of love, it means that we can love the person we don't like. This is not a matter of the reaction of the heart; it is an attitude of the will and the whole personality deliberately directed to the other man. You cannot order a man to fall in love in the romantic sense of the term. Falling in love is like stepping on a banana skin; it happens, and that is all there is to it. But you can say to a man: 'Your attitude to others must be such that you will never, never, never want anything but their highest good.'
>
> Source: William Barclay, 'Situation Ethics', Chapter 4 in his *Ethics in a Permissive Society* (Collins, 1971), pp. 69–91; reproduced with permission

Exam tip

Remember, questions asking you to clarify the ideas in a set text will only occur in the A-level paper (Section B, question 3a). You are *not* required to answer this question type in your AS examination.

(e) The command word 'Clarify' requires you to show knowledge and understanding of the ideas that are outlined in the question and are presented in the passage (AO1). In this question, the passage quoted will always be drawn from the *Anthology.*

You are asked to explain how the ideas in the passage help someone to understand the situation ethicist's understanding of love.

You should spend 15 minutes answering the 'Clarify' question.

Student answer A

The concept of love is prevalent in situation ethics. The passage distinguishes between three types of love — philia, storge and agape love. He makes it clear that agape is unconditional love. Situation ethics argues against legalism and antinomianism, and agape is thus the middle way between the two. He then argues that we should do the most loving action, and that includes loving the person we don't like. a This suggests situation ethics is a very positive theory and that we should treat everyone and every situation with the same loving attitude. b

(e) **Level 2 awarded.**

a The answer demonstrates limited knowledge about situation ethics' understanding of love. The extract is summarised and simplified without a clear analysis of the argument. The reference to legalism and antinomianism is not obviously relevant. b There is no indication here of any wider understanding. In answering this question, the student should make it clear that he or she has read and understood the fuller extract contained in the *Anthology*, and drawn from that understanding to shed light on the given extract.

Student answer B

William Barclay is a well-known critic of situation ethics. In this extract from *Ethics in a Permissive Society*, he outlines the principle of agape love and the difference between agape and other types of love. This passage shows that love takes different forms. There is love experienced by sexual partners (eros); the love between friends (philia), for example a friend helping another with their work; love within a family, for example a mother choosing to breastfeed her baby. In situation ethics, the key idea of love is agape. a This is 'unconquerable goodwill', which refers to the fact that, as humans, we should always do the most loving thing for others, regardless of who they are or what they have done for us. This is crucial because it means we should love our enemy. Barclay reasserts that agape love is purpose, not passion; there is no spontaneity about it, like falling in love. Agape love is an attitude, not a feeling, which means it is about living by the principle of love in order to choose the most moral course of action, that is, achieving the highest Good. Breaking established rules and principles in order to achieve this highest good is sometimes necessary, but this is moral if it is done out of love. b

ⓔ Level 3 awarded.

ⓐ This response analyses clearly all the key aspects of the passage: the distinction between the different types of love and why agape love is so central to situation ethics. **ⓑ** It also considers the implications of the argument, in that it considers why situation ethics could be regarded as an effective ethical theory. The response therefore accesses the marks for knowledge and understanding as it correctly explains the key aspects of situation ethics and references the extract clearly.

■ Question 3b: Analyse

Question 3b

Analyse the strengths and weaknesses of situation ethics as an approach to ethical decision-making.

(20 marks)

ⓔ The command word 'Analyse' requires you to 'deconstruct information and/or issues to find connections and provide logical chains of reasoning in order to make judgements regarding their importance/relevance to the question context'.

There are 5 marks available for demonstrating knowledge and understanding (AO1) and 15 marks for evaluation (AO2). You should focus primarily on discussing the merits and problems associated with the ideas outlined in the question.

In this example, the principal task is to discuss the strengths and weaknesses of situation ethics as an ethical theory, with a particular focus on whether it can help us make moral decisions, and by extension whether it can give us clear moral guidelines and solve moral dilemmas. To achieve level 3 would require making reference to both the weaknesses and the corresponding strengths of situation ethics, demonstrating a broad understanding and presenting a balanced argument.

In the A-level exam you should spend about 30 minutes on your answer.

> **Exam tip**
>
> 'Analyse' is both an AS and A-level command word, with questions always worth 20 marks. On the AS exam paper, question 4b will use the command word 'Analyse'. On the A-level paper it will be question 3b as here. However, only A-level questions will be based on a section of text from the *Anthology*. This sample question is taken from the A-level only part of the specification. In the AS exam you should spend about 20 minutes on your answer to question 4b.

Student answer A

Ethics are the moral principles that govern a person's behaviour. John Robinson published a book called *Honest to God* in 1963 in which he argued that we should see God as a part of our lives instead of as a distant being. He also argued that religion has to change in order to respond effectively to atheism and the liberalisation of society. However, William Barclay in *Ethics in a Permissive Society* (1971) argues that situation ethics gives humans too much responsibility, and that humans might not make the correct decision in certain situations. Therefore, although situation ethics tries to make itself compatible with our modern society, whether it is a religious theory or not is debatable because it doesn't really fit in with traditional religion, only with modern religion.

Situation ethics argues that you should 'love your neighbour as yourself'. This love is greater than any other love, and is an attitude rather than a feeling. Robinson and Fletcher argue that agape should be the rule that defines situation ethics. One implication of agape is that there is nothing immoral about divorce. However, Roman Catholics would argue that divorce is immoral. Situationist thinking is developed by Fletcher who argues that the Church follows legalism, following strict commands rather than seeking to fulfil agape. [a]

Fletcher gives very extreme examples to justify his point, for example a prisoner of war who gets pregnant or a man who stops taking his medication so that his family can benefit from his life insurance. His argument doesn't work in day-to-day life; moral rules work better. [b]

Overall, situation ethics is not a very effective theory of ethics even though the fundamental principle of agape is arguably derived from Christian morality.

[e] **Level 3 awarded.**

This is quite a brief and simple analysis of the strengths and weaknesses of situation ethics. [a] There is a chain of reasoning but points are not developed or precise enough. [b] There is an attempt to appraise evidence but it is quite limited. It is very important to give examples and justify any evaluative claim you make.

Student answer B

Situation ethics is based upon the principle of agape and provides a middle way between the absolute, definite rigidity of legalism and the disregard for moral rules of antinomianism. However, situation ethics is regarded by figures such as William Barclay as being irresponsible as a theory of ethics as it can justify immoral actions and go against the Christian values that the theory is based on. [a]

Barclay claims that situation ethics allows a degree of freedom as people are given the capacity to choose between moral principles and their own judgement in cases where they feel that principles need to be put aside. However, Barclay describes this freedom as terrifying as he considers it to be a licence to do what you want, rather than what is moral and recommended by scriptures. A situation ethicist response comes from Robinson who states that 'man has come of age' and that humans are rational enough to make their own decisions. Fletcher, too, argues that situation ethics is not breaking rules for its own sake, but is arguing that moral rules should be followed unless they clearly are not the most loving thing to do — that is, they do not follow the rule of agape. Fletcher also refers to working principles, that is positivism, relativism and pragmatism.

Fletcher gives key examples where it does make sense to use agape as the guiding moral principle. In one of them, he tells the story of a prisoner of war who decides to become pregnant by a prison officer, knowing that the pregnancy will mean she will be able to return home to her husband and children. While it is clear that adultery is seen as morally wrong, in this case, based on agape love, this is the most moral decision as it means her family can be reunited with her. Barclay, however, finds Fletcher's examples too extreme, and says that such actions should not be condoned in less exceptional circumstances. b

Barclay argues that there is something profoundly unchristian about situation ethics and considers the theory gives too much responsibility to humans who don't know how to act or make appropriate decisions. Situation ethics ignores that the Bible is a source of authority for Christians and this is why the theory has been rejected by the Roman Catholic Church and the majority of the Anglican community. Situation ethics has been criticised as it does not reflect New Testament views on morality, especially on theft and adultery. Barclay further argues that man has not come of age and that society needs rules in order for people to lead moral lives. Fletcher, however, argues that Jesus himself was a situation ethicist and followed the rule of agape; when necessary, he rejected established moral and religious laws.

To conclude, while situation ethics could be criticised on the basis that it can at times justify what we would regard as immoral actions, it only does so in cases where established moral principles, especially religious ones, would not be the most loving thing to do. c

e Level 5 awarded.

a The 5 marks for AO1 are achieved through the use of key terminology and an accurate analysis of situation ethics. b The reasoning is coherent and logical, and evaluative points are supported by evidence. c A clear conclusion is provided, which takes into account both sides of the argument. This answer is comprehensive enough to be in the top band as there is a good range of evaluative points on both sides.

■ Question 4: Evaluate (A-level only)

Question 4

Evaluate the view that abortion should be considered moral.   (30 marks)

ⓔ The command word 'Evaluate' requires you to review and analyse information, bringing it together to form a conclusion or judgement based on strengths/ weaknesses, alternatives, relevant data or information.

In this question, you are being asked to consider the morality of abortion from a variety of perspectives. You should mention characteristics of personhood and quality vs sanctity of life arguments as well as secular and religious approaches to the question.

Because it is an 'Evaluate' question, you are also required to come to a supported judgement, meaning you should conclude the essay by offering an opinion about where the balance of judgement lies — whether abortion should be considered moral, in some or all circumstances.

Of the 30 marks available, 5 marks are awarded for knowledge and understanding (AO1) and 25 marks for evaluation (AO2). Your knowledge and understanding will be demonstrated indirectly when you evaluate the issue raised.

Alongside Religion and Ethics you will have studied Philosophy of Religion and either New Testament Studies or Study of Religion. *In your response to this question, you must include how developments in Religion and Ethics have been influenced by either Philosophy of Religion or one of the other areas of study.* In this answer you must also show how ideas from one of these subject areas can be linked to your discussion of this question, otherwise your mark will be capped at level 4. Any links made do not need to be detailed.

With a total of 30 marks available for this question, you may want to spend about 40–45 minutes answering it.

Exam tip

Note that you will be required to answer an 'Evaluate' question in the A-level examination only. It will appear as question 4 in Section C of the exam paper. AS students will not be expected to answer an 'Evaluate' question.

Student answer A

An abortion is the deliberate termination of a human pregnancy; most are performed during the first 28 weeks of pregnancy. There are many ethical reasons why people oppose abortion.

One argument for abortion is that a foetus does not have any characteristics of personhood. A foetus lacks rationality, language, self-awareness and beliefs and is merely a potential person. It is thus not entitled to the same rights and liberties that persons have and terminating the life of a potential person can still be classified as moral as it does not hold the qualities of an actual person. ⓐ

However, religious views such as the Roman Catholic view would oppose the idea of abortion due to the sanctity of life argument. This is the idea that human life at any stage is sacred and God-given and therefore only God has the right to give and take life. This is a weakness of the view that abortion should be considered moral. b

On the other hand, rules around the practice of abortion are strictly regulated. An example of this is that two doctors must consent to the abortion taking place before it occurs. However, it could be argued that this normalises abortion, leading to a slippery slope argument.

Deontology considers abortion immoral because killing an embryo or a foetus cannot be universalised, as it would lead to no children. c

The philosopher Judith Jarvis Thomson understands abortion to be moral. She argues that having an abortion is simply denying an embryo or a foetus the right to have a womb to develop in. Feminist arguments align with Thomson's view and are in favour of the pro-choice argument. d However, Thomson's argument (which makes an analogy between pregnancy and being kidnapped and hooked on to a machine tied to another person) raises the issue of consent in sexual relationships and the outcome of an unwanted pregnancy. It doesn't work as well in cases where sex is consensual and no contraception is used or if a woman changes her mind or is pregnant with a foetus who has severe health issues. e

ⓔ Level 3 awarded.

a Knowledge and understanding are present but the discussion is limited in scope. There is some evidence of synoptic links with b Christianity and c ethical theory but the answer needs to be more scholarly.

Examiners want to read answers which are organised and logical. In this case, there is a clear structure, as each paragraph considers a specific approach to the problem posed, but there isn't a clear narrative or a logic to the order of arguments, following through either by issue or by philosophical approaches. d It is just listing different positions.

e There is no judgement and no real appraisal of evidence, which means it cannot reach level 4 or 5.

Student answer B

The quality of life argument argues that, in the modern world, we should consider whether all life has value and whether a person is suffering to the point where they feel it is not worth living. In the case of abortion, we need to consider the quality of life of the woman but also the possible suffering of the child to be born. A woman who is pregnant and is considering an abortion may feel that her quality of life would be reduced if she would miss out on education and would struggle to cope with a child. Due to medical advances, doctors are able to terminate pregnancies using safe, quick and convenient methods. a

Some people, however, believe that life starts at conception. Therefore a problem with adopting the quality of life approach on abortion is that it permits the killing of a potential person. The embryo contains the potential to develop into a conscious, self-aware being capable of having desires about its future. This is what Don Marquis argues: an abortion deprives a being of a future and it is therefore immoral.

However, Judith Jarvis Thomson disputes this idea that an abortion is a violation of the right to life of a potential person. She sets out the scenario of a woman who suddenly wakes up one morning to find an unconscious violinist connected to her circulatory system: he has a fatal kidney ailment and needs the woman's kidneys to filter his blood. He will die if he is disconnected but will recover fully if he stays connected for nine months. For Thomson this scenario mirrors a case of pregnancy. In the same way that the violinist has no right to the woman's body as she has not consented to it, the foetus has no rights to the use of a woman's body: it is the woman's choice to control what happens to her body. This supports abortion because it concludes that women are not obliged to carry a child for nine months while suffering physical and emotional strain. A woman who does so is more like a Good Samaritan going above and beyond for another, because being a mother is not every woman's life-given purpose or duty.

However, this argument is not very strong because in most cases of pregnancy, women voluntarily engage in sexual intercourse, aware of the risk of becoming pregnant. Although this point could be countered by the fact that people who use contraception go out of their way to prevent conception, no form of contraception is 100% safe. Therefore consensual sex is also consenting to the possible conception of an embryo and is not the same as being kidnapped and plugged on to another human against your will, as the scenario suggests. **b**

The sanctity of life argument takes a different approach. It argues that life is created by God which makes it intrinsically good. This sacred gift can only be given and taken away by God. The argument thus gives a clear-cut answer to the problem of abortion: it is immoral. This links to natural law theory, which takes the Christian perspective that rational beings should follow natural law and what is moral can be determined on the basis of primary precepts. For example, the primary precepts of reproduction and not killing mean that the purpose of sexual relationship is procreation. However, there are issues with this argument because it argues that all cases of abortion are wrong because the embryo or foetus has rights regardless of the conditions in which it is created; these could involve rape or incest. It also disregards the fact that a sick child could have a very poor quality of life and would suffer all its life. An even more significant problem is in cases where the woman could become ill or even die as a result of the pregnancy. However, some religious believers use the doctrine of double effect to resolve some of those issues. For example, if the woman is suffering from an ectopic pregnancy whereby the embryo grows in her fallopian tube rather than in her womb, then doctors would remove her fallopian tube to save her but that would carry the unintended consequence of killing the embryo. This solution works in cases where a woman's life is at risk but not really in cases of rape or incest. **c**

The solution may be to use situation ethics as the basis to make decisions on abortion. Fletcher talks about love as agape love which is about loving other people as yourself and can involve self-sacrifice. That means that having an abortion in the case of incest or rape could in some situations be the most loving thing to do because of the trauma for the woman; the child too could have a very poor quality of life, but it would be the woman's decision. In other cases, continuing with the pregnancy, despite some hardships, could be the most loving thing to do as it would mean taking into account what is best for the woman and for the future child. d

Therefore the debate on the morality of abortion is complex and there can never be a 'yes' or 'no' answer: we should consider each case on its own merits. While some religious believers argue that abortion is immoral because life is sacred, in some cases an abortion can be the most loving thing to do and prevents unnecessary suffering. e

e Level 5 awarded.

a This is a detailed answer which shows both depth and breadth, is scholarly and understands the wider significance of this difficult issue. b A variety of arguments is analysed and evaluated, and clear links to other areas of religious studies (c Christianity and d situation ethics) are embedded in the essay, preserving the logic of the argument. e There is also a clear conclusion which answers the question.

Knowledge check answers

1 This is an area of philosophy concerned with the moral relationship between humans and their environment and with humanity's duties and responsibilities towards the environment. This has grown in importance because of the impact of technology, rising populations and pollution.

2 Dominion relates to the view that humans have God-given mastery of the natural world. Stewardship implies a duty of care; we must look after and protect the natural world.

3 Deep ecology is an ecological and environmental philosophy which argues that all living things have inherent worth regardless of their instrumental utility to humans. Shallow ecology is the belief that the value of non-human organisms is extrinsic, instrumental to the benefit of humankind, rather than an end in itself.

4 Animals are objects of moral concern because they feel pleasure and pain.

5 We are all made in the image of God and God loves us all equally, irrespective of gender, race, ability, sexual orientation and so on. Everyone does not have to be treated the same, but they must be treated fairly.

6 Historically, Christians have fought against slavery. Martin Luther King used his Christian faith and status in the black community to change attitudes and policies towards black people in 1960s' America.

7 Hedonism is the pursuit of pleasure.

8 Human nature is about self-interest — the desire to maximise pleasure and minimise pain.

9 On the basis of the principle of utility — the tendency of the act to produce the greatest good for the greatest number.

10 Yes. Despite the adoption of moral rules, rule utilitarianism shares with act utilitarianism the view that human nature is about self-interest: we naturally seek pleasure and avoid pain.

11 Selfless, unconditional love.

12 Both take account of the consequences of actions and argue that the end justifies the means.

13 An example could be separation of conjoined twins, where one twin would not survive the surgery. Divine command theory would reject this as murder. The situationist would argue that agape means you should save the life that can be saved.

14 The secondary precepts are specific rules to be obeyed. They are absolute and their aim is to guide us on how to live.

15 Natural law would argue that all three are morally wrong because they go against the primary precepts of procreation, preserving life and, in the case of divorce, living in an ordered society.

16 It takes possible consequences into account when making moral decisions.

17 A paratrooper and a guerrilla fighter are clearly combatants. An injured pilot is a non-combatant. An army chaplain is considered a non-combatant because theirs is a supporting role. Child soldiers are considered combatants, however, which might surprise you.

18 It could be justified in self-defence, or to defend liberties and rights. In his case study on the atomic bomb, Joseph Fletcher suggests that war may sometimes be the lesser of two evils.

19 On the one hand we could argue that the existence of nuclear weapons prevents war as parties are more likely to use diplomacy with countries which have nuclear weapons. This fits in with the principles of *jus ad bellum* which aim to prevent war unless absolutely necessary. On the other hand, the use of nuclear weapons and the mass damage they produce make it impossible to distinguish between combatants and non-combatants. There is also an issue with proportionality as the damage inflicted is not proportionate to the cause.

20 Marriage for Catholics is sacred. It means two people becoming one through divine union. The purpose of sex is to reproduce.

21 Jack Dominian's argument goes against the principles of natural law. Under natural law, a sexual relationship can only take place in the context of marriage between a man and a woman. For Dominian, love is more important than such principles. Hence, he doesn't condemn divorce or homosexuality.

22 Liberal Protestantism broadly follows the principles of situation ethics, i.e. an ethics of tolerance grounded in agape love. Liberal Christians do not consider divorce, homosexuality or contraception immoral because what matters first is a loving relationship. They also argue that IVF is moral on the basis that bringing a child into the world is the most loving thing to do. Evangelical Christians, however, argue that sex should only take place within marriage between a man and a woman, on the basis that this is what the scriptures advocate. They argue that homosexuality is a sin, but agree with Liberal Protestants on the morality of IVF. However, they do condemn surrogacy. Evangelical Protestants don't see contraception as wrong if used in marriage, as sex is for pleasure as well as procreation.

23 Moore argues that the question of defining the Good is an open rather than a closed question. If I ask 'Is the Good pleasure?' (using Mill's definition of the Good), the answer cannot be a simple 'yes' or 'no' as it would be to a closed question. There is never a definite answer in the way that questions like 'Are all bachelors unmarried men?' can provide us with one. The Good is not naturally understood to be pleasure. The naturalistic fallacy is committed whenever we define the Good in natural terms: thus because we use the word 'good' with reference to something else, we think the word 'good' is identical to that

second term. For example, we may describe something pleasant or pleasurable as 'good', but this doesn't mean we should infer that 'good' means 'pleasant' or 'pleasurable'.

24 Ethical naturalism argues that the Good is a natural property of the world: it is a psychological property — for J. S. Mill it is pleasure. Moore disagrees and argues that the Good doesn't equate to and cannot be reduced to pleasure. Instead the Good is an intuition, a non-natural property of the world which exists but cannot be defined.

25 Hume argues that statements about reality (what is) are fundamentally different from statements about morality (what one ought to do). We cannot deduce an 'ought' from an 'is'. I cannot derive from the fact that some people kill others that killing is wrong. I derive the value 'killing is wrong' from my emotional response to acts of killing in the world (my aversion to it, my own fear of being killed).

26 Emotivism is a non-cognitivist position arguing that nothing is inherently right or wrong. A moral statement is just an expression of emotion; there is no moral truth and therefore no possibility of moral progress. Even if values change, the newer values are morally no better or worse than those they replace.

27 Emotivism is a non-cognitive theory of ethics because it argues that moral language is meaningless. Ethical statements are neither true nor false; they do not say anything about the world but merely express a subjective emotional reaction.

Similarly, prescriptivism denies any objective truth and claims that moral language doesn't represent the world; there are no moral properties in the world. When we make an ethical statement we are prescribing our opinions and giving imperatives for others to follow.

28 Either (i) God is the source of all good and therefore whatever God commands becomes good; or (ii) God commands us to do things because they are 'good'. In either case, the conclusion poses a threat to the theist idea of God. If (i) is true, the Good simply becomes what God wills as opposed to what is truly right or wrong; he could will wrong actions, i.e. is not omnibenevolent. If (ii) is true, this implies that God is conforming to an independent standard of goodness so he cannot be omnipotent.

29 What both organisations have in common is an intolerance of other ways of life and of other religious groups. They support patriarchy and argue that abortion and contraception are evil even if the woman's life is at risk. These positions make them a minority among Christians but support Sharpe's view that religion doesn't necessarily advocate morality and can justify what most would regard as immoral actions, on the grounds that the type of behaviour and moral code they defend promotes intolerance or inequality or leads to harm.

30 The first formulation of the categorical imperative focuses on universalisability: personal maxims are moral if they can be made universal without contradiction. For example, killing is immoral because it would lead to a contradiction in conception: if killing was moral, we would all kill each other and there would be no one left to kill — which is contradictory.

The second formulation of the categorical imperative focuses more closely on how we treat other human beings. We should treat other people not just as a means to an end but as an end as well — that is, with equal respect and dignity.

31 Agent-neutral reasons apply to all moral agents: every agent has the same aims. Utilitarianism is agent-neutral as it claims that the aim of every moral agent is to achieve happiness.

Agent-relative reasons apply to specific moral agents: different agents have different aims. Moral reasons are subjective: it is about what drives the agent.

32 The highest good is happiness and this is linked to acting according to reason. It is rational to want to perform your function well. Virtues are forms of action in accordance with reason.

33 The good life is the interaction between intellectual or practical wisdom (phronesis) and virtuous actions which results in a virtuous character. This moral development allows us to flourish and achieve eudaimonia.

34 We are born without character; character develops over time. It is shaped and moulded through practice. This will take many years because it is a practical discipline.

35 It is important because being a person means having a moral status and deserving moral consideration when it comes to matters of life and death.

36 For Roman Catholics and natural law, personhood starts at conception: embryos and foetuses have human rights. Preventing them from developing as nature intended is depriving them of a future. Embryonic stem cell research and PGD are therefore morally wrong.

37 Ordinary or proportionate medical treatment (e.g. the provision of food or water or pain relief) is useful to the goal of the restoration of health and gives reasonable hope of benefit, which outweighs any adverse effect. Extraordinary or disproportionate treatment (e.g. the administration of a new or experimental therapy in some instances) is medical treatment that offers no reasonable hope of benefit and/or involves a grave burden on the patient and their family.

Note: **bold** page numbers indicate key term definitions.

Index

Index